Federal Tax Treatment
of Income
from Oil and Gas

Federal Tax Treatment

of Income

from Oil and Gas

STEPHEN L. McDONALD

A background paper prepared for a conference
of experts held October 18-19, 1962, together
with a summary of the conference discussion

Studies of Government Finance

THE BROOKINGS INSTITUTION

WASHINGTON, D.C.

Foreword

THIS VOLUME ON THE TAX treatment of income from the production of oil and gas is the third Brookings publication in a series of studies sponsored by the National Committee on Government Finance, and it is the second of this series stemming from the Conference Program of the National Committee. The volume contains the background paper prepared for a conference of experts, sponsored by the Brookings Institution and held in Washington October 18–19, 1962, and a summary of the discussion at the conference.

The tax treatment of income from oil and minerals is one of the most controversial issues in federal taxation. The distinctive tax provisions applying to this industry are justified by its proponents on several grounds. They argue that there are unusual risks in oil and mineral exploration and development; that depletion and exploration and development allowances are needed to finance new discoveries; and that the present provisions offer a strong incentive for taxpayers who discover new sources of oil and minerals to operate these properties rather than to sell them for a profit that would be taxed at the preferential capital gains rate. Critics of these provisions believe that they lead to overinvestment in the preferred industries and hence tend to result in a serious misallocation of resources; that the risk in these industries would be satisfactorily handled by the general deductibility of losses; that the oil and mineral industries are no more strategic from a national defense standpoint than many others; and that the present provisions relating to these industries are highly inequitable.

It was not the purpose of the conference of experts to agree on specific policy recommendations. Rather, the purpose was to explore through frank and competent discussion certain major economic issues. The report of the discussion in Chapter 10 of this book, it is hoped, will help clarify the issues and improve understanding of some of the recent discussion of this subject in the technical literature.

The thirty-four participants in the conference, who are listed on pages 139–40, represent various shades of opinion on the tax treatment of the oil and gas industry. They were selected by the Brookings Institution on the basis of background, experience, and ability to contribute to a discussion of the technical issues in this field. They were invited in their personal capacities and not as representatives of the organizations with which they are affiliated.

The background material and conference summary were prepared by Stephen L. McDonald of the University of Texas. Since this study is intended to open issues for full discussion rather than to draw firm conclusions about them, it places special obligations and restraints upon the author. He must entertain as much as he can of what might be relevant, regardless of his opinion as to actual relevance, and he must at least mute the expression of his own strongly held belief. Even with these restraints, Professor McDonald has made a contribution to a difficult subject.

In preparing the background study for publication, Professor McDonald made slight revisions to reflect factual material developed since the study was first written—material which might significantly affect the interpretation of certain of his arguments. The principal revision pertains to the use of empirical data in his analysis of the effects of distinctive tax treatment of the oil and gas industry on the allocation of resources. No revisions were made in the background study where they would affect the pertinence of the reported conference discussion of particular issues.

For their helpful comments and suggestions, the author is indebted to Ruth Rasch, Martin J. Bailey, W. J. Crawford, Douglas H. Eldridge, Charles O. Galvin, Richard J. Gonzalez, Richard Goode, Robert G. James, Richard J. Kruizenga, Warren A. Law, Joseph Lerner, Richard A. Musgrave, and Joseph A. Pechman. He is especially grateful to Dr. Pechman, who organized the conference and made numerous helpful suggestions on the background paper and summary chapter.

The National Committee on Government Finance was established in 1960 by the trustees of the Brookings Institution to supervise a comprehensive program of studies on taxation and government expenditures. The Studies of Government Finance are supported with funds provided by the Ford Foundation.

The views expressed in this study are those of the author and do not purport to represent the views of the National Committee on Government Finance or the staff members, officers, or trustees of the Brookings Institution.

ROBERT D. CALKINS
President

October 1963
The Brookings Institution
1775 Massachusetts Ave., N. W.
Washington, D. C.

Studies of Government Finance

Studies of Government Finance is a special program of research and education in taxation and government expenditures at the federal, state, and local levels. These studies are under the supervision of the National Committee on Government Finance appointed by the Trustees of the Brookings Institution, and are supported by a special grant from the Ford Foundation.

MEMBERS OF THE ADVISORY COMMITTEE

Contents

List of Tables

CHAPTER I

Introduction and Summary

THIS STUDY OFFERS an exploratory examination of the distinctive tax treatment accorded by the federal government to income from oil and gas production. Its purpose is to lay the foundation for a more exhaustive discussion and analysis of the economic issues by suggesting analytical approaches and summarizing available pertinent data.

In the United States two distinctive tax provisions apply to income from oil and gas production.[1] First, the tax-return deduction for depletion of oil and gas must be computed for each producing property as the larger of (1) a *pro rata* fraction of the capitalized costs of the property or (2) $27\frac{1}{2}$ percent of the gross value of the production, not to exceed 50 percent of the net income, of the property during the tax period. The former method of computing allowable depletion ("cost depletion") permits deductions over the life of a producing property that total no more than actual investment outlays. The latter method ("percentage depletion") permits total deductions that exceed actual investment outlays. Second, oil and gas producers may either (1) capitalize dry hole costs and the intangible costs of drilling productive wells and recover them through cost depletion or (2) treat them as ordinary current operating expenses,

[1] See *Internal Revenue Code of 1954*, Secs. 611–16.

deductible for tax purposes in the tax periods in which they are incurred. If the expensing option is exercised, allowable percentage depletion is affected, if at all, only through the limitation to 50 percent of net income. It is readily apparent that the general effect of percentage depletion and the expensing of major capital outlays (explained more fully in Chapter II) is to tax income from oil and gas production at lower rates than apply to most other income.

The differential federal tax treatment of income from oil and gas production raises a number of issues, among them the following: (1) the alleged greater risk involved in the oil and gas industry, (2) the appropriate way to measure periodic consumption of "wasting assets," (3) the need to conserve oil and gas resources, (4) national defense considerations, (5) use of the capital gains device in combination with the distinctive tax provisions, (6) the probable effect on price of any change in the rate of percentage depletion, and (7) the effects on tax revenue of a change in the rate of percentage depletion. The analysis of these issues is briefly summarized below.

Risk and Resource Allocation

The standard economic criticism of the distinctive tax provisions applying to income from oil and gas production is that, by reducing the effective income tax rate in the industry relative to that in other industries, the provisions induce an uneconomical allocation of resources to the search for and production of oil and gas. The relative prices of oil and gas thus tend to be reduced, and more oil and gas is consumed, relative to other products of the economy, than is consistent with maximizing satisfactions from total available resources.

This argument assumes that the corporation income tax is in no degree shifted, and it abstracts from differences in risk and capital intensity among industries. There appears to be some basis for regarding as relatively risky and capital intensive that phase of the oil and gas industry to which percentage depletion and other distinctive tax provisions apply. On the basis of the combined influences of presumed high risk and capital intensity, a case can be made for differentially low rates of taxation of income from oil and gas production, where the comparison is with the "typical" manufacturing firm. The case assumes that a tax on the return to capital is shifted in the long run and rests on the premise that tax neutrality with respect to the allocation of resources is economically desirable. Unfortunately, the data required to make a satisfactory test of the neutrality of existing distinctive tax provisions are not available.

Percentage Depletion and Discovery Value Depletion

The oil and gas industry differs from most others in that there is ordinarily little relation between *specific* exploration and development outlays and the value of the oil and gas acquired as a result of those outlays. It is possible—even likely—that investors may make some capital outlays in the search for oil and gas without receiving sufficient income from oil and gas and other sources to get the full benefit of the tax deduction allowed for such outlays. The result is to overstate the industry's total taxable income and thus to overtax that income unless the more successful investors are permitted to take deductions that exceed their actual outlays. Assuming that total industry capital outlays tend to equal total values acquired through discovery and development effort, if discovery value were used as the basis for determining the rate of depletion allowed, the results would approximate those obtained in industries where outlays and values acquired are initially similar in each individual case. Percentage depletion was originally conceived as a substitute for discovery value depletion, and the deductions allowed under percentage depletion may still closely approximate those that would be allowed under discovery value depletion. But if percentage depletion is justified on these grounds, one must logically argue that deductions for discovery outlays actually made should not be allowed. With minor qualifications, however, the current percentage depletion deduction allowed is in addition to deductions for discovery outlays actually made.

Conservation

Whether or not the distinctive tax provisions applying to income from oil and gas production are in themselves in the interest of oil and gas conservation defined in an economically meaningful way depends upon the effects of these provisions on general resource allocation. If they are neutral, that is, if they merely keep the prices of oil and gas relative to other prices from being altered by the income tax, then they are in themselves consistent with conservation. In this case, they do not arbitrarily alter the allocation of investment between the intensive margin of exploitation and the extensive margin of search for new deposits determined by current prices, the rate of interest, and expectations of future prices and costs.

If the distinctive tax provisions are not neutral, they are in themselves inconsistent with conservation, because then they do arbitrarily affect the distribution of effort between recovery from existing deposits and the search for new deposits. However, the effects of the tax provisions are modified by the prevailing pattern of state conservation regulation, which tends to place undue emphasis on recovery from existing deposits and to induce wastefully large investments in oil field development. The conservation effects of the distinctive tax provisions may in some part be offset by opposite effects of state conservation regulation. If differential taxation tends to underprice oil and gas currently, there may be no undue expansion of exploration relative to recovery, the cost saving of relatively low taxation being dissipated in the wasteful applications of labor and capital associated with devices of state conservation regulation.

National Defense

The distinctive tax provisions applying to income from oil and gas production may further the national security by helping to create and maintain either reserve domestic capacity or divertible domestic capacity. In the absence of the prevailing devices of state conservation regulation, particularly the restriction of production to market demand and the exemption of marginal wells from restriction, the tax provisions themselves would not contribute to a persistent excess capacity in the industry. A policy of artificially stimulating the consumption of oil and gas, in order to create and maintain capacity that would be divertible to military use in time of national emergency, is questionable on three grounds: (1) initially "marginal" uses would tend with time to become "essential"; (2) the policy would hasten the exhaustion of domestically discoverable deposits, and (3) other industries that might be equally essential to national defense would have to bear a heavier tax burden than would otherwise be necessary. That the distinctive tax provisions contribute to national security in either of the above two ways is, therefore, highly doubtful. If the tax provisions are neutral in their effects on the allocation of resources, however, they are consistent with the kind of general economic efficiency that is itself in the interest of national security.

The Capital Gains Device

The capital gains device, combined with the distinctive tax provisions, has several interesting effects: It increases the profits on successful investments in oil and gas exploration and development by "outsiders" in high marginal tax brackets by allowing them to pay no more than a 25-percent tax on realized income after having taken deductions for outlays at higher effective rates. It allows firms and individuals who can find suitable buyers of productive properties to escape forever some of the income tax liability that was apparently only postponed by earlier expensing of unsuccessful exploration and intangible development costs. If the percentage rate of depletion allowed were reduced or eliminated, use of the capital gains device by owners of modest-sized producing interests and firms would limit the resulting overall increase in the industry's income tax liability to the Treasury. For many firms and individuals, the capital gains alternative is a close substitute for percentage depletion. Unless the capital gains alternative were at the same time modified appropriately, reduction or elimination of the percentage depletion allowance would have little adverse effect on the economic incomes of such firms and individuals.

Price Effects

Reducing or eliminating percentage depletion would tend to raise the absolute and relative prices of oil and gas by imposing additional costs on production and discouraging investment in new discovery and development effort. Under present circumstances in the industry, however, much if not all of the increased tax burden might be absorbed through cost reductions, principally by increasing output relative to capacity and reducing lease bonuses paid for new prospects. Costs might be reduced also by eliminating excessive drilling in development, but such reductions, requiring prior legislative and regulatory action, would not necessarily follow from reduction or elimination of percentage depletion. In the very long run—of say ten to fifteen years—much of the increased income tax burden resulting from a change in the rate of percentage depletion could be shifted back to landowners (recipients of economic rent) in the form of reduced lease bonuses and royalty payments.

Revenue Effects

Tax revenues of all governments taken together would probably be increased if percentage depletion were reduced or eliminated. However, the size of the gain is most unpredictable in the present state of knowledge, for it would depend on how the industry adjusted to its increased effective income tax rate and the degree to which the capital gains device was used to avoid additional income tax liability. Under the most favorable circumstances, with restrictions on the use of the capital gains alternative and industry adjustment by means of cost reduction, total revenue gains might go as high as $2 billion annually. Under less favorable circumstances, with the capital gains alternative used extensively and industry adjustment primarily in the form of price increases, total revenue gains might be limited to a few hundred million dollars annually.

There are several reasons why the conclusions reached here are not in themselves an adequate basis for an income tax policy with respect to the oil and gas industry: (1) The analysis is limited to economic issues and runs in purely economic terms. No effort is made to evaluate present or alternative tax policies in terms of general public policy, equity, or international politics, for instance, although such considerations are necessary for a full evaluation. (2) Some of the analysis is novel. Until the analytical devices used have been examined more thoroughly than they are here, the conclusions reached must be regarded as tentative. (3) In some instances the available data are quantitatively or qualitatively insufficient to permit satisfactory tests of hypotheses. And (4) not all of the possible economic issues relating to distinctive tax provisions are considered. For instance, no effort is made to assess the possible effects of these provisions on the international allocation of oil and gas productive activity. Although such allocation is pertinent to national defense and the domestic price of petroleum, the matter is so intermixed with noneconomic considerations, and usable relevant data are so scarce, that it was deemed most fruitful for the present purposes to focus on the domestic scene.

CHAPTER II

Distinctive Tax Provisions Applying to Oil and Gas

DOMESTICALLY EARNED INCOME from oil and gas production (as defined for tax purposes under existing federal statutes and regulations) is subject to the same rates of taxation, given the nature and size of income of the taxpayer, as is domestically earned taxable income from any other source. The distinctive tax provisions applying to income from oil and gas production pertain to the *definition* of current income for tax purposes; that is, they pertain to the amount and timing of deductions that the affected taxpayer may make from his gross receipts in determining his taxable income.

Description of Provisions

These provisions, all involving a possible alternative by the affected taxpayer, are: (1) the percentage depletion allowance, (2) the expensing of intangible development costs as incurred, and (3) the expensing as incurred of dry hole and certain other costs of unsuccessful exploration effort. The first provision relates to the amount that the affected taxpayer may deduct from his gross receipts, both for a given tax period and in total, as representing capital consumption in the form of depletion of assets through the extraction and sale of oil and gas. The other two provisions relate chiefly to the timing of deductions that reflect actual outlays by the taxpayer, although, as will be shown below, they are not unrelated to the percentage depletion provision. Of course, all of them are concerned with the principle prevailing in American income taxation that taxable income is gross receipts less the legitimate costs of acquiring those receipts, including the consumption of capital.

Cost Depletion and Percentage Depletion

The current income tax law[2] provides that the deduction for consumption of capital through depletion of oil and gas deposits in a given tax period shall be computed for each productive property as the larger of (1) a *pro rata* (unit-of-production) fraction of the capitalized costs of the property, or (2) $27\frac{1}{2}$ percent of the gross value of the production, not to exceed 50 percent of the net income, of the property during the tax period. The former alternative is known as cost depletion. To compute the appropriate cost depletion deduction for a given year, the adjusted cost basis of the property which would be used to determine the gain upon its sale is divided by the total units to be produced over the remaining life of the property, estimated as of the beginning of the year, and the result is multiplied by the number of units produced and sold during the year. It is readily apparent that if the cost depletion method is used throughout the life of a productive property, the periodic tax deductions sum up to the initial capitalized cost of the property (less any salvage value, of course).

The second alternative indicated above is known as percentage depletion. Under this alternative, the total tax deductions that result are in no way limited by the initial capitalized cost of the depletable asset and generally exceed this amount. Either the cost depletion or the percentage depletion alternative is available to all who have direct ownership shares in the minerals being produced, including owners of royalties and various "carved-out" shares in production.[3] Owners of indirect interests, such as shareholders or

[2] See U. S. Congress, Joint Economic Committee, *The Federal Revenue System: Facts and Problems, 1961* (Government Printing Office, 1961), pp. 89–93, for a summary of current provisions with respect to income from natural resources.

[3] For definitions and examples of the various possible economic interests in oil and gas production, see Charles O. Galvin, "The 'Ought' and 'Is' of Oil-and-Gas Taxation," *Harvard Law Review*, Vol. 73 (June 1960), pp. 1,477 ff.

creditors of corporations owning oil and gas properties, have no right to any sort of depletion deduction from the income they receive from such interests.

Intangible Development Costs

The second distinctive provision applying to the taxation of income from oil and gas production pertains to the so-called intangible costs of drilling productive wells and preparing them for production, often called "intangible development costs." Examples of such costs are expenditures for labor, fuel, power, materials, supplies, tool rental, and repairs of drilling equipment in connection with drilling and equipping productive wells.[4] (Tangible development costs include such costs as expenditures for pipe, tanks, and pumps.) The taxpayer has the option of either capitalizing intangible development costs and recovering them through cost depletion or writing them off as a current expense.[5] If he chooses the latter alternative, his allowable deductions under the percentage depletion option are not reduced, unless the intangible development costs currently expensed are large enough to bring into operation the 50-percent-of-net rule limiting the percentage depletion deduction.[6] Needless to say, the taxpayer ordinarily finds it in his interest to deduct intangible development costs as current expense.

Dry Hole Costs

Finally, the taxpayer who has elected to capitalize intangible drilling costs has the further option of capitalizing dry hole costs and recovering them through cost depletion or of expensing them as incurred. As with intangible development costs, it is ordinarily in the interest of the taxpayer to expense dry hole costs as incurred, since the percentage depletion deduction is thereby affected, if at all, only through the 50-percent-of-net limitation. Other costs of exploration effort found to be unsuccessful may likewise be written off as current expense or ordinary loss.[7]

[4] Joint Economic Committee, *op. cit.*, p. 91.

[5] If the taxpayer chooses to expense intangible development costs, he must thereafter use that method for all his properties.

[6] *Ibid.*, pp. 91–92. See also the explanation of the application of distinctive tax provisions below.

[7] *Ibid.*, p. 91. For a more precise explanation of the treatment of exploration costs other than dry hole costs, see items 3 and 4 in Table 1.

History of the Distinctive Provisions

A brief account of the evolution of the distinctive tax provisions applying to income from oil and gas production may clarify the nature of the issues to be discussed below. The transition from cost to discovery value to percentage depletion in the years 1916–26 reveals a problem largely peculiar to mineral industries, especially oil and gas: that of defining and measuring the capital value to be recovered through depletion deductions in cases where the individual taxpayer's outlays on capital account do not necessarily have any close relation to the value of the assets acquired. Also light may be thrown on the current relation of the expensing of intangible development costs to allowable percentage depletion by reviewing the way in which the two provisions evolved through different channels of lawmaking.

The absence of any reference in the following historical sketch to legislative and public controversy over distinctive tax provisions in the oil and gas industry does not mean that there was none. On the contrary, discussion of these provisions over the years has always excited disagreement. But since the issues are to be discussed in detail below, only a bare recital of the evolutionary steps, with brief comments relating them to issues later to be discussed, is given here. Moreover, only where legislative intent is stated in the record or is clearly implied in the form of action taken is an attempt made here to link successive steps with explanations. Even in such cases it must be recognized that the record is subject to different interpretations, particularly since the motivations of individual lawmakers are not necessarily the same as the legislative intent formally stated or implied by the Congress.

The history of percentage depletion[8] and related provisions begins, of course, with the Sixteenth Amendment to the Constitution,

---

[8] The following account is based on *Legislative History of Depletion Allowances*, U. S. Congress, Joint Committee on Internal Revenue Taxation, 81 Cong. 2 sess., Committee Print (1950); F. J. Blaise, "What Every Tax Man Should Know About Percentage Depletion," *Taxes: The Tax Magazine*, Vol. 36 (June 1958), Appendix, pp. 417–26; and Oscar H. Lentz, "Mineral Economics and the Problem of Equitable Taxation," *Quarterly of the Colorado School of Mines*, Vol. 55 (April 1960), pp. 10–27. Galvin, *op. cit.*, pp. 1,458–59, note 48, cites a number of additional sources.

finally ratified in February 1913, which authorized federal income taxation as we know it today. In the first implementing legislation, the Revenue Act of 1913, Congress recognized the need to provide rules governing deductions for capital consumption. The Act authorized "a reasonable allowance" for capital consumption and, in the case of mines (including oil and gas wells), specified a maximum permissible depletion deduction of 5 percent of the gross value at the mine of output during the tax period.

The Revenue Act of 1916 made no distinction in principle between mining and other types of enterprises in the rules governing deductions for capital consumption. It provided for depreciation or depletion, as the case might be, based on costs, or, in the case of capital assets held prior to March 1, 1913, the fair market value as of that date. It is perhaps significant for later developments that the rule implied a recognized distinction between the cost and the capital value of an asset, even though in this case the intent seems to have been to put those who acquired capital assets prior to March 1, 1913 (when costs and prices were materially lower) on a cost basis similar to that of those who acquired assets more recently. The rule probably had particular value to discoverer-owners of highly productive mineral properties, since even immediately upon discovery, cost and capital value of individual properties need have little relation to each other. Thus, in the case of mineral properties, a taxpayer may have chosen depletion based on fair market value as of March 1, 1913, rather than cost, not because of a change in the price level after acquisition, but because of a significant discrepancy between cost and value fortuitously acquired through discovery.

In the Revenue Act of 1918, depletion based on cost or on the March 1, 1913 value was retained. However, the significant provision was added that, in the case of mines and oil and gas wells discovered by the taxpayer on or after March 1, 1913, and not acquired by purchase, if the fair market value was "materially disproportionate" to the cost, the basis of depletion could be discovery value. Under the discovery value method of computing depletion deductions for tax purposes, the capital sum to be recovered was the fair market value of newly discovered deposits. Fair market value was defined as that which would be agreed upon by a willing buyer and a willing seller under the circumstances prevailing during a period of thirty days following discovery. Discovery value depletion was thus based on the estimated capital value of minerals in the ground. Both the statement of the Senate Finance Committee[9] and the restriction of its application to properties acquired through discovery by the taxpayer indicate that the primary aim was to provide a special incentive for exploration. Since capital gains were then treated as ordinary income, the special incentive provided was similar for discoverer-sellers and discoverer-operators of mineral properties. Undoubtedly the oil and gas industry was more affected than most other mineral industries by this provision, because of the need for continuing exploration even to maintain a given level of oil and gas ouput for extended periods.[10]

In the Revenue Act of 1921 discovery value depletion was limited to 100 percent of a property's net income computed without allowance for depletion. The purpose of this provision was to preclude charging off tax losses from mineral operations against taxable income from other sources. The Revenue Act of 1924 tightened the limitation to 50 percent of a property's net income before depletion.

The administration of discovery value depletion in the case of oil and gas properties proved exceedingly difficult, involving in many instances lengthy investigation, negotiation, and litigation in determining fair market values. Apparently to eliminate this difficulty and at the same time perpetuate discovery value depletion in principle, the Congress undertook in 1926 to substitute a rule-of-thumb measure for allowable oil and gas depletion deductions. This was to be based on the typical relation of discovery value deductions to gross income in the years preceding. Although the House and Senate proposed different figures for this relationship, the Conference Committee compromised on $27\frac{1}{2}$ percent, and the provision was passed into law. In the 1926 legislation, the 50-percent-of-net limitation was retained, as was the alternative of using cost depletion if it provided a larger deduction than did percentage depletion, but an important change was made in the extent of its application.

[9] Joint Committee on Internal Revenue Taxation, *op. cit.*, p. 2.

[10] In other mineral industries, the feasible rate of production is generally unaffected by the degree of depletion of known deposits. Moreover, known deposits in such industries are usually larger relative to current output than is the case with oil and gas. Exploration activity proper thus tends to bear a smaller ratio to current production activity in such industries, and, in some instances, to be quite discontinuous.

Discovery value depletion had been inapplicable to income from properties acquired by purchase, but percentage depletion was made applicable to income from all oil and gas production. Percentage depletion was thus less specifically an exploration incentive device than discovery value depletion had been, a fact that did not go unnoticed by opponents of the 1926 legislation.[11]

Only one change of any significance has been made in the general approach to oil and gas depletion deductions adopted in 1926. The Revenue Act of 1932 provided that the basis of cost depletion be adjusted downward for depletion actually allowed, whether cost depletion or percentage depletion. Before that time a taxpayer could use percentage depletion without reducing his cost basis—an advantage if he later wanted to sell an affected property or shift to cost depletion.

Unlike the percentage depletion provision, which evolved through the legislative process, the option to expense intangible development costs and the costs of unsuccessful exploration effort developed through administrative decisions and regulations.[12] Pursuant to the Revenue Act of 1916, as amended by the Revenue Act of 1917, Treasury Decision 2447 was issued in February 1917, providing that the "incidental expenses of drilling wells," expenses that "do not necessarily enter into and form a part of the capital invested or property account," might, at the option of the taxpayer, be deducted from gross income as ordinary operating expenses. Internal Revenue Regulation 33, Revised, issued in January 1918, used similar language, further providing that costs charged to capital account under the option and "represented by physical property" might be recovered through depreciation (as distinguished from depletion). Regulation 33 also provided specifically that the cost of drilling unproductive wells could be treated as an ordinary operating expense. Subsequent regulations and decisions, their issue dates running into the 1950's, retained the provision regarding dry hole costs and, in the case of productive wells, gradually extended the term "incidental expenses of drilling" to embrace all expenditures for items of an intangible nature.

[11] Joint Committee on Internal Revenue Taxation, *op. cit.*, p. 10.

[12] The following paragraph is based on Galvin, *op. cit.*, pp. 1,465–69; and Lentz, *op. cit.*, pp. 29–31.

As early as 1933, however, the Treasury firmly established that capitalized intangible development costs (except those incurred in installing casing and equipment and in constructing derricks and other physical structures) were recoverable through depletion, and not through depreciation. It was not until 1945 that the Congress took any official cognizance of the question of intangible development costs. In that year the Fifth Circuit Court of Appeals cast a shadow on the validity of the Treasury regulations on such costs by stating that the administrative rulings had gone beyond statutory authority. Congress at once passed a concurrent resolution expressing its approval of existing Treasury regulations and, in the Revenue Act of 1954, embodied this approval in the statutes.[13]

The history of the percentage depletion provision indicates that it was intended to be an administratively more feasible equivalent of discovery value depletion, although not restricted to discoverer-taxpayers as discovery value depletion had been. The latter recognized that, due to the uncertainties of exploration, the values of deposits discovered might substantially exceed costs of discovery. It was adopted to provide a special incentive to exploratory activity by allowing the taxpayer the higher of two depletion bases. Logically, then, discovery value depletion (hence percentage depletion) is an alternative to depletion based on costs. But, with a minor exception to be noted below, the use of discovery value (or its supposed equivalent, percentage depletion) did not (and does not) preclude the additional deduction from gross income of nearly all of the actual outlays of explorers in making discoveries and preparing their properties for production. Indeed, as the rules have been administratively developed, in a sense independently of the statutory law, most

---

[13] The 1954 Code, Section 263 (c), provides that ". . . regulations shall be prescribed . . . corresponding to the regulations which granted the option to deduct as expenses intangible drilling and development costs in the case of oil and gas wells and which were recognized and approved by the Congress in House Concurrent Resolution 50, Seventy-ninth Congress." Although this language would seem to clarify the authority of the Internal Revenue Service to make the questioned regulations, failure of the Congress to embody the regulations themselves in the statute leaves uncertain the exact current status of the regulations as between administrative and statutory law. For opposing legal interpretations, see Harrop A. Freeman, "Percentage Depletion for Oil—A Policy Issue," *Indiana Law Journal* (Summer 1955), p. 408 (holding that the regulations are still not statutory); and W. Leo Austin, "Percentage Depletion; Its Background and Legislative History," *University of Kansas City Law Review* (Fall 1952), p. 29, both cited by Lentz, *op. cit.*, p. 31.

exploration[14] and development costs are deductible as operating expenses and hence are subject, as it were, to super-accelerated amortization. The basis of the controversy over percentage depletion and related tax provisions thus becomes obvious.

Application of the Provisions

To understand the practical application of percentage depletion and related provisions, it is important first to know the tax accounting treatment of various types of costs involved in finding and producing oil and gas. Table 1 provides a summary. It will be noted that most items of cost are deductible from gross income either as current operating expense or as depreciation. The right to these deductions is unaffected when the discoverer-taxpayer uses percentage depletion instead of cost depletion. However, two kinds of costs are affected when he elects to use percentage depletion. Capitalized lease acquisition costs and capitalized exploration costs attributable to producing properties are deductible *as such* only through cost depletion. The taxpayer may not deduct from his gross income *both* percentage depletion and the *pro rata* amount of capitalized lease acquisition costs and capitalized exploration costs.

Relative Advantages in Cost and Percentage Depletion

The sacrifice may be large or small, depending on the circumstances under which he acquired his interest in the property.[15] For discoverer-producers who are continuously active in both production and exploration for new deposits, and who are successful in the

[14] Here and elsewhere, unless otherwise indicated, the term "exploration costs" includes dry hole costs.

[15] For example, if the operator purchased the property after a discovery had been made on it, his initial cost basis would be relatively large. If he made his own discovery after having leased the property under terms involving a small lease bonus, his initial cost basis would be relatively small. The term "sacrifice" used in connection with the statement that the taxpayer may not deduct *both* percentage depletion and a *pro rata* amount of capitalized lease acquisition costs and capitalized exploration expenses should not be interpreted to mean that the taxpayer is deprived of the right to recover his full costs. Rather, percentage depletion substitutes for the specific deduction of such costs from gross income. Hence the net benefit of percentage depletion is reduced to the extent of the taxpayer's initial cost basis.

TABLE 1. Tax Accounting Treatment of Expenditures in the Finding, Development, and Production of Oil and Gas

Expenditure	Tax Treatment
1. Dry hole costs	1. Expensed as incurred[a]
2. Lease rentals	2. Expensed as incurred
3. Lease acquisition costs	3. Capitalized upon acquisition
a. Leases later proved unproductive	a. Capitalized cost charged off as loss upon surrender of lease[b]
b. Leases later proved productive	b. Capitalized cost recoverable as such only through cost depletion
4. Other exploration expense (such as geophysics, geology)	4. Capitalized if on an area of interest,[c] otherwise expensed as incurred
a. Areas later proved unproductive	a. Capitalized costs charged off as a loss upon surrender of property[b]
b. Areas later proved productive	b. Capitalized cost recoverable as such only through cost depletion
5. Intangible drilling costs of producing wells	5. Option of expensing as incurred or capitalizing and recovering through cost depletion[d]
6. Tangible equipment on producing wells	6. Capitalized and recovered through depreciation
7. General lease equipment on producing properties	7. Capitalized and recovered through depreciation
8. Production costs	8. Expensed as incurred

[a] Taxpayers electing to capitalize intangible drilling costs have the additional option of either expensing or capitalizing dry hole costs. The option to capitalize intangibles is almost never used.

[b] Or upon final determination of worthlessness of mineral rights without immediate surrender of the property.

[c] An area of interest is one in which further exploratory work is at least conditionally contemplated.

[d] Capitalized intangible costs incurred in the installation of casing and equipment and in the construction on the premises of derricks and other physical structures are recoverable through depreciation.

long run, the sacrifice probably is not very large, possibly amounting typically to as much as 3 percent of gross income.[16] Consequently, percentage depletion, together with other deductions for capital consumption and expense, usually allows the oil and gas dis-

[16] Entirely representative statistical evidence to validate this figure is lacking. However, such evidence as is available indicates that the figure given is not unreasonable as an upper limit. The most recent Treasury Department survey of corporate depletion deductions pertains to the years 1950, 1951, and 1952. The number of companies represented in the oil and gas industry sample averaged only 100 for the three years, but these companies accounted for almost exactly 90 percent of total oil and gas industry corporate depletion deductions for the period. The sample average allowable depletion was 25.3 percent of gross income from extraction. Of allowable depletion, 95.7 percent, on an average, was excess over cost basis depletion. The indicated "sacrifice" of cost basis deductions is thus 1.1 percent of gross income from extraction. (U. S. Treasury Department, Office of Tax Analysis, "Statistics of Corporation Mineral Depletion De-

coverer-taxpayer greater total deductions from gross income for tax purposes than the actual finding, development, and production costs of the minerals from which the income is earned. Moreover, a great part of the finding and development outlays may be treated as operating expenses and hence are recoverable without delay.[17] Percentage depletion and related provisions, therefore, offer a financial advantage to the affected taxpayer. How great the advantage is depends on: (1) the excess of percentage depletion deductions over those that would be possible under cost depletion, (2) the proportion of total outlays that may be treated as operating expenses, and (3) the rate at which the taxpayer discounts future income.

The percentage depletion deduction is computed on the basis of the gross income of each individual producing property.[18] For lessees, this gross income is exclusive of royalties paid.[19] As stated above, the taxpayer may deduct for depletion as much as $27\frac{1}{2}$ per-

---

ductions and Related Allowances, 1950, 1951, and 1952" [mimeo.], March 10, 1955, pp. 29, 37–40.)

On the basis of a sample of 31 companies whose domestic production ranged from less than 7,000 barrels a day to more than 300,000 barrels a day in 1957 and collectively accounted for 47 percent of total domestic production in that year, Peter O. Steiner found that capitalized exploration costs not subject to recovery in addition to percentage depletion averaged about 2.9 percent *of total finding and development costs* in the years 1955–57. ("Percentage Depletion and Resource Allocation," *Tax Revision Compendium*, Vol. 2, papers submitted to U. S. Congress, House Committee on Ways and Means, Committee Print [November 1959], p. 960.) A nationwide survey indicates that finding and development costs averaged slightly less than 70 percent of gross income from production in the years 1948, 1951, 1953, and 1955. (Mid-Continent Oil and Gas Association, *Percentage Depletion, Economic Progress, and National Security* [Tulsa, 1961], p. 34, citing C. C. Anderson, Chief Petroleum Engineer, U. S. Bureau of Mines, "Petroleum and Natural Gas in the United States—Relation of Economic and Technologic Trends," paper presented to World Power Conference, Montreal, Sept. 7–11, 1958.) If this percentage is combined with the Steiner finding, it is indicated that capitalized exploration costs not subject to recovery in addition to percentage depletion are in the neighborhood of 2 percent (2.9 × 70 percent) of gross income from production.

[17] Steiner (*op. cit.*, p. 960) found that, for the period 1955 through 1957, between 60 and 64 percent of total finding and development costs incurred by the companies in his sample were written off against income in the year incurred.

[18] A property is defined generally as "each separate interest owned by the taxpayer in each mineral deposit in each separate tract of land." However, two or more separate operating interests constituting an "operating unit" may be aggregated and treated as a single property, whether or not they are included in a single tract or parcel of land or in contiguous tracts or parcels of land. (*Internal Revenue Code of 1954*, Sec. 614.)

[19] Of course, royalty owners are entitled to percentage depletion (or cost depletion, if they so elect) on their share of total production.

cent of each property's gross income as defined. However, the deduction may not exceed 50 percent of the net income attributable to the property—the property's gross income less all of the allowable expenses attributable to it. The percentage depletion deduction is then 27½ percent of the property's gross income after royalties or 50 percent of its net income, whichever is smaller.

Assume now a lessee firm operating two productive properties, as in Part A of Table 2. Although the two properties have the same gross income after royalties, Property B is allowed a depletion deduction of only $20,000 due to the 50-percent-of-net limitation, while Property A is allowed $27,500, the full 27½ percent of gross income. Note that the costs attributable to the properties include the cost of dry holes drilled on them and the intangible expenses of drilling productive wells on them. Therefore, in some instances the expensing of finding and development outlays may be competitive with, rather than supplementary to, the percentage depletion deduction. Given the level of production costs proper on particular productive properties, the full benefits of percentage depletion may be received in some instances only if the deductions for intangible development costs plus the costs of dry holes drilled on those productive properties are small. On the other hand, up to the point where deductions for such outlays begin to compete with the percentage depletion deduction, the operator may save current tax dollars by increasing his expenditures on development drilling.

Effect of Percentage Depletion on Income Tax Liability

The distinction between properties is significant only for determining the total allowable depletion for the firm. The firm's income tax liability is based on the consolidated net income derived from the two properties after an additional deduction for business costs not attributable to either property. Computation of the income tax liability of the hypothetical firm is illustrated in Part B of Table 2. It will be noted that costs of unsuccessful exploration (including dry hole costs) not attributable to productive properties, being irrelevant to the computation of allowable depletion, are not competitive with percentage depletion. Up to the point where taxable income becomes zero, such expenses permit tax deductions that definitely supplement percentage depletion. While no operator

TABLE 2. Computation of Allowable Percentage Depletion Deduction
and Federal Income Tax Liability, Hypothetical Firm "X"

A. Allowable percentage depletion deduction

	Properties	
	A	B
Gross income after royalty.............................	$100,000	$100,000
Less: Costs attributable to property[a]....................	40,000	60,000
Net property income before depletion..................	60,000	40,000
(27½% of gross)...............................	(27,500)	(27,500)
(50% of net)...................................	(30,000)	(20,000)
Less: Allowable depletion............................	27,500	20,000
Net property income after depletion..................	32,500	20,000

B. Federal income tax liability

	Both properties consolidated
Gross income after royalty...	$200,000
Less: Costs attributable to individual properties.......................	100,000
Net property income before depletion..............................	100,000
Less: Allowable depletion deduction...............................	47,500
Net property income after depletion...............................	52,500
Less: All other costs of doing business[b].............................	22,500
Net taxable income...	30,000
Less: Federal income tax[c]...	10,100
Net income after tax per tax return...............................	19,900

[a] Covering production expenses (including production taxes and an apportionment of overhead), ad valorem taxes, allocable interest, depreciation of tangible well investment, cost of dry holes drilled on the property and intangible expenses of drilling productive wells. They exclude lease acquisition and capitalized exploration costs attributable to the property.
[b] Including cost of dry holes not attributable to producing properties, other exploration expenses, cost of surrendered leases, lease rentals, interest and taxes not allocable to producing properties, and overhead and miscellaneous expenses attributable to nonproducing properties.
[c] Thirty percent of the first $25,000 plus 52 percent of the amount over $25,000.

would deliberately incur expenses on exploration that he knew
would be unsuccessful, the current deductibility of unsuccessful exploration expenses is germane to capital budgeting and might in

some instances induce a firm anticipating income tax liability on current operations to increase its exploratory drilling.

In the hypothetical example, the total depletion deduction is $47,500, which is about 23.8 percent of gross income, as compared with the maximum allowable rate of 27½ percent.[20] Suppose the firm might have taken deductions amounting to $7,500 based on capitalized lease acquisition costs and capitalized exploration costs attributable to the producing properties (which, it will be recalled, cannot be additionally deducted from gross income under the percentage depletion option). The allowable depletion deduction would then exceed the alternative cost basis depletion by $40,000 ($47,500 minus $7,500), or 20 percent of gross income.[21] That is, the total deductions from gross income for tax purposes would exceed by $40,000 the total costs actually incurred by the firm and attributable to the income period. It is this excess, rather than the actual

[20] The hypothetical example in Table 2 is designed to illustrate, among other things, the effects upon total allowable percentage depletion of the 50-percent-of-net limitation. With each productive property or "operating unit" (see note 18) treated separately for purposes of computing allowable depletion, the limitation has the effect of holding the total percentage depletion deduction for the aggregate of all affected properties below the 27½ percent maximum whenever any one or more properties cannot receive the maximum percentage depletion. The disaggregation rule in computing percentage depletion is thus usually a disadvantage, as compared with complete aggregation, to the taxpaper. Disaggregation may be an advantage, however, when the taxpayer has one or more properties whose net incomes are small enough (perhaps negative) to make cost depletion for such properties the more attractive alternative. With disaggregation, the low or negative net incomes on some properties do not pull down the maximum allowable percentage depletion on other properties. The total allowable depletion (cost depletion on some properties and percentage depletion on others) may thus in some instances be larger than if all properties were aggregated for purposes of computing the allowable percentage depletion.

[21] The illustrative percentages indicating the effective depletion rate and the effective rate of allowable depletion in excess of cost basis are believed to be reasonably close to the industry experience. A publication of a major oil company states without explanation: "In recent years the *effective* depletion rate of the oil industry in the United States has averaged about 23 percent." (Standard Oil Company of New Jersey, *An Analysis of the Depletion Provision as it Applies to the Petroleum Industry* [New York, 1958], p. 3. Italics in original.) The effective depletion rates in the Treasury sample previously mentioned, about 25 percent (see note 16), are probably somewhat too high to be currently representative of the industry as a whole because of the nature of the sample (large corporations only). On the other hand, it should be noted that current property aggregation rules are more permissive of high average effective depletion rates than the rules prevailing in 1950–52. (See note 18.)

depletion deduction, that measures the advantage of percentage depletion to the firm.

The firm's internal accounts would, of course, reflect this benefit. Specifically, on account of the excess of allowable depletion over cost basis depletion, the firm's financial net income after taxes, as it would be reported on the basis of conventional accounting practices to management and stockholders, would be $59,900 rather than $19,900 as indicated on the tax return. The effective income tax rate would be about 14.4 percent, rather than the nominal 33.7 percent approximately. In short, the effect of percentage depletion may be viewed as a reduction (though not necessarily in the degree illustrated here) of the effective tax rate applying to income from oil and gas production.

Effect of Expensing Option on Income Tax Liability

INTANGIBLE DEVELOPMENT COSTS. For most firms in the oil and gas industry, intangible development costs give rise to another discrepancy between tax return and internal accounting statements of net income after taxes. For their own accounting purposes, most firms capitalize intangible development costs and amortize them over the life of the productive properties to which they relate.[22] Nearly all firms expense such costs, however, for tax return purposes. Accordingly, in the case of the typical growing firm (whose development outlays tend to rise from year to year), tax return deductions for current intangible development costs ordinarily exceed current charges for amortization of intangible development costs. The difference is reflected in a corresponding excess of reported financial net income after taxes over tax-return net income after taxes.

DRY HOLE COSTS. The expensing of dry hole and other costs of unsuccessful exploration is a somewhat different matter. In this case, conventional accounting practice in the industry generally corresponds with tax-return practice. However, the successful, growing firm tends to understate its current net income (and its current net worth) as a result. For a firm that is a going concern and for the in-

[22] Horace R. Brock, "Accounting for Leasehold, Exploration and Development Costs in the American Petroleum Industry," (unpublished doctoral thesis, The University of Texas, 1954), p. 309.

dustry as a whole, unsuccessful exploration costs are an inevitable part of the total costs of acquiring productive assets and are economically chargeable against the output of productive assets as production occurs. To charge current unsuccessful exploration costs to current production is, in a successful, growing firm, to understate current income by an amount equal to the excess of expensed outlays over that portion of past unsuccessful exploration outlays economically attributable to current production. Also understated by the same amount is the current addition to assets resulting from exploration effort.[23] It is true, of course, that capitalizing and amortizing unsuccessful exploration costs would involve very arbitrary accounting techniques. This is because there is, for this category of costs, no specific property with a productive life over which to spread the capitalized costs. Hence, the expensing of unsuccessful exploration costs is not an altogether unreasonable accounting practice. However, in a growing firm it does understate current income by charging against current receipts costs that are in excess of those economically attributable to such receipts.

Expensing vs. Amortization of Costs

There are two aspects to the question of expensing intangible development costs and unsuccessful exploration costs. One concerns an economically meaningful statement of current income, which is pertinent to the interpretation of accounting records. The other concerns the relative economic benefits of expensing instead of capitalizing and amortizing. The two are related, but they are not the same thing. To illustrate, assume that a firm makes constant annual outlays for productive assets that are qualitatively similar and have a productive life of ten years. If the firm expenses its outlays as they occur, during the first ten years it understates its economic income, but thereafter, so long as it maintains the outlays, it correctly states its economic income. If it should cease making outlays for

---

[23] There is no entry for oil and gas reserves on the balance sheet of an oil and gas producing firm. *Capitalized* investment outlays appear there as symbolic of oil and gas (and other assets) acquired through investment outlays. It is well known by those familiar with the industry, including investment analysts, of course, that one must have independent estimates of oil and gas reserves to place a realistic value on the net worth of a producing firm.

productive assets, the firm would overstate its economic income for ten years, after which time all its assets would be consumed. The understatement in the first ten years would exactly match the overstatement in the last ten years, so that over the complete cycle hypothesized the firm would accurately state its total income. If there is an income tax with a constant rate, the absolute dollar tax saving resulting from capital consumption deductions is the same, over the complete hypothesized cycle, whether the firm expenses its outlays on capital account or capitalizes them and amortizes them over the productive life of the asset. But the economic effect is not the same, of course. If the firm should expense its outlays for income tax purposes, its tax bill would be lower in the first ten years and correspondingly higher in the final ten years. In effect, a portion of the lifetime tax bill is deferred. The amount of economic benefit to the taxpayer depends on the amount of tax deferred, the period of deferment, and the opportunity cost of capital to the firm.

For example, suppose that for an indefinite period a firm makes annual outlays on capital account of $100, these outlays and the corresponding capital consumption deductions being spread evenly over each of the assumed ten years of asset life. Assume the effective income tax rate to be 50 percent and the firm's opportunity cost of capital to be 20 percent a year. The alternative to expensing outlays for tax purposes is assumed to be straight-line amortization. In the first year, the firm's straight-line amortization deduction would be $5 (the average amount invested for the period being $50); in the second year, $15, etc., through $95 in the tenth year.

By expensing its outlays, the firm would increase its capital consumption deduction by $95 the first year, $85 the second year, etc., through $5 in the tenth year. Its net tax saving through expensing would accordingly be $47.50 ($95 × .50) the first year, $42.50 the second year, etc., through $2.50 in the tenth year. Through the first ten years, the firm's net tax saving on account of expensing would total $250. If the firm maintains its annual outlays of $100, it neither adds to nor diminishes this deferred tax obligation of $250. Even though it no longer understates its current income, it has the use of $250 more than if it had been using straight-line depreciation for tax return purposes. If capital is worth 20 percent a year to the firm, as assumed, the firm's earnings are larger than they otherwise would have been by $50 ($250 × .20) a year.[24] The $250 tax deferment accumulated in the first ten years may be regarded as an interest-free loan from the Treasury to the firm, a loan which may be renewed each year that the firm maintains its outlays at $100. If the firm should ever cease making outlays on capital account, it would, in effect, repay the "loan" over the ensuing ten-year period.

It should be clear from the foregoing that if a firm's outlays on capital account grow indefinitely, then expensing rather than amortization over productive asset life would mean understating its current income indefinitely. The amount of tax deferred would grow indefinitely. Each year the Treasury would, in effect, renew and add to its outstanding "loan" to the growing firm. The firm would automatically qualify for the "loan" renewal and augmentation by replacing consumed assets and purchasing others in addition.

The benefits of expensing as compared with amortization may also be measured in terms of the relative present values of the resultant tax savings. Assume an opportunity cost of capital (discount rate) of 20 percent a year and an effective tax rate of 50 percent. A capital outlay of $100 *immediately*[25] deducted from current income for tax purposes, results in a tax saving having a present worth of $50. If the same outlay is recovered over a ten-year period through straight-line amortization, the present worth of the tax saving is approximately $25. Expensing thus provides a *net* saving to the taxpayer equal to one-fourth [($50 − $25) ÷ $100] of the original outlay. Expensing the outlay rather than amortizing it thus reduces the cost of the asset by one-fourth. The effect is less, of course, if one compares expensing with amortization by use of a formula more usual in industrial depreciation than the straight-line formula. For example, ten-year amortization according to the "double-declining-

---

[24] This implicit interest income of $50 would be realized in the eleventh year and thereafter, so long as outlays remained constant at $100 a year. Of course, implicit interest in smaller amounts would be earned by the firm on the gradually increasing tax deferment during the first ten years; and if the deferred balance should ever decline, on the remaining deferment in the declining years.

[25] Immediate deductibility is assumed for simplification. To make the other present worth computations strictly comparable, the first year's amortization is likewise assumed to be deductible at the time the outlay is made.

balance" formula[26] results in tax savings whose present worth, discounted at 20 percent a year, is about $30. In this case expensing thus provides a *net* saving of approximately one-fifth the initial outlay.

Even with a discount rate of 10 percent, the advantages of expensing over amortization are quite significant. At this rate the present worth of tax saving through ten-year straight-line amortization of $100 is approximately $34. Under the double-declining-balance method, the present worth is about $38. Expensing thus provides a *net* saving of 16 percent of the outlay in the first case and 12 percent in the second case.

Conclusion

Especially for successful, growing firms, percentage depletion and the expensing of the greater part of current costs of exploration and development form an effective tax-saving package—so effective that there have been many significant examples in the postwar period of firms going for extended periods with little or no income tax liability.[27] It is important to emphasize, however, that it is the package, and not simply percentage depletion, that can produce this result; and then only for rapidly growing firms. The influence of the growth factor can be seen (Table 2) if it is assumed that all outlays for lease rentals, exploration, and development cease in the hypothetical firm. In such circumstances, percentage depletion could result at best in cutting taxable income in half, in view of the 50-percent-of-net limitation. Even so, the great significance of percentage depletion in the package is apparent. It always accounts for a large portion of the possible tax saving, and it is an absolute tax saving not dependent upon the effect of timing for its value.

[26] The "double-declining-balance" formula is:

$$\text{Annual deduction} = \frac{2 \times \text{remainder to be amortized}}{\text{original useful life in years}}.$$

For amortization of $100 over ten years, the first year's deduction is $20, the second $16, etc. The nature of the formula requires a switch to straight-line or some other definitely exhausting formula in the last few years of the time period. In the examples in the text, straight-line amortization is used in the seventh through the tenth years.

[27] Senator Paul Douglas of Illinois compiled and placed in the record of Senate debate a list of 27 "horrible examples." *Congressional Record* (Senate), Vol. 103 (Mar. 27, 1957), p. 3,978.

CHAPTER III

Differential Risk

ECONOMIC RISK IS AN EXPRESSION of the chances of loss in an economic undertaking. Loss is defined as the failure of the income from the undertaking to be as large as that reasonably expected and necessary in the long run to justify undertakings of the same sort. To illustrate, when an investor makes an outlay on capital account, he presumably expects to derive from it a stream of income[28] that will yield some positive rate of return on the capital employed. If it is absolutely certain that the expected income will be received, then the investment may be said to be completely riskless. If, on the other hand, there is some possibility that the realized rate of return will be smaller than that expected, then the investment is to that extent a risky one. The greater the possibility that the realized rate of return will fall short of the expected rate, the greater the economic risk associated with the investment.

The same principle may be stated somewhat differently. Given his alternatives (which include simply holding idle funds), a potential investor will have in mind at a given time minimum rates of return that different investments must yield in order to attract his funds. He will consider a particular project if the reasonably expectable flow of income from it, when discounted at the appropriate

[28] The "income" in question is net cash flow, i.e., gross cash proceeds less cash expenses, and not net income in the ordinary meaning of the term.

minimum acceptable rate of return, has a present value that is at least equal to the investment outlay initially required. If there is absolutely no chance that the realized present value could differ from the investment outlay, then the project is utterly riskless. There is risk, however, to the extent that there is a possibility of an unfavorable discrepancy between realized present value and investment outlay.

The concept of economic risk implicitly postulates that for a given investment project there is a certain probability distribution of possible rates of return or realized present values. Risk may be defined more precisely, then, in terms of the dispersion of the possible return on investment around the most probable (and most reasonably expected) value,[29] the degree of risk varying directly with the degree of dispersion.[30]

Risk and Uncertainty

Most writers follow the classical distinction of Knight[31] between risk proper and uncertainty. According to Knight, risk proper pertains to a situation of known probabilities. Where probabilities are known, the chances of loss are theoretically "insurable"; that is, by making a sufficiently large number of investments having the known probability distribution of possible results, an investor may insure that the aggregate result of these investments will approximate the most probable result in the distribution. This, of course, is the principle underlying the life, property, and casualty insurance businesses.

Uncertainty, in contrast, is a concept expressing decision makers' ignorance about the probability distribution of possible

[29] For examples of this definition authoritatively used in contemporary literature, see Joel Dean, *Managerial Economics* (Prentice-Hall, 1956), p. 7; and James W. McKie, "Market Structure and Uncertainty in Oil and Gas Exploration," *Quarterly Journal of Economics*, Vol. 74 (November 1960), pp. 554–55.

[30] With positive dispersion, there is the possibility of skewness in the probability distribution of possible investment results. The presence of skewness precludes a simple relationship between degree of dispersion and degree of risk. For instance, two distributions having identical degrees of dispersion, but one exhibiting negative skewness and the other positive skewness, would undoubtedly be differently evaluated by prospective investors. One may note also that "the most probable value" is ambiguous in the presence of skewness.

[31] Frank H. Knight, *Risk, Uncertainty and Profit* (Houghton Mifflin, 1921).

results from a given investment project. Such ignorance may arise out of temporary inexperience with a new but given set of forces. In the more significant case, however, it arises out of a constantly changing set of forces, so that the experience with any particular investment or group of investments does not provide a reliable basis for predicting results from other, outwardly similar, investments. Under such circumstances, it is impossible in effect to assemble a large number of projects having the same probability distribution of possible results and thus insure the aggregate result. Where uncertainty prevails, the outcome of even a very large number of outwardly similar investment projects cannot be confidently predicted.[32]

Practically speaking, the distinction between risk proper and uncertainty is one of degree. One can think of no businesses in which investment results are perfectly predictable. (The risks of a gambling house are not confined to the gaming tables.) On the other hand, it is doubtful that any investor (including any business management) is ever wholly lacking in experience and information that would throw some light on the possible distribution of results from even an entirely new type of investment. It is probably safe to say, therefore, that all investments are made with the chance that realized results will differ from expected results; yet they are made with some idea of the reasonably expectable result and the range of possible results. In the discussion to follow the conceptual distinction between risk and uncertainty will be used where appropriate. In general, however, the convenient and familiar terms "risk" and "riskiness" will be used to indicate the possibility of discrepancy between expected and realized investment results.

Sources of Risk

Risk in business may arise from several sources and apply to several different phases of business operations. For example, the property used in the business may be accidentally or deliberately destroyed; the equipment and processes involved may be rendered

---

[32] Cf. the distinction between risk and uncertainty of Nicholas Georgescu-Roegen, "Choice, Expectations and Measurability," *Quarterly Journal of Economics*, Vol. 68 (November 1954), p. 524, cited in McKie, *op. cit.*, p. 555n.

obsolete by technological innovations carried out by others; products may become obsolete or otherwise inferior in the public mind as the result of improved knowledge or of competitors' improvements and inventions; costs of inputs may rise unpredictably, and product prices may fall unpredictably; instability of income, due to general business fluctuations or other uncontrollable causes, such as variations in growing conditions in agriculture, may jeopardize a firm's ability to meet fixed obligations and remain solvent; population movements or the unexpected exhaustion of specific natural resource deposits may make a business poorly located for continued profitable operation; a business may be declared illegal or made subject to onerous and expensive regulation; a business may be burdened with unanticipated differential taxation or otherwise be required to assume some cost (e.g., that of waste disposal) not contemplated in the original investment decision. For the most part, these risks are beyond insurability in the usual sense of the term. Strictly speaking, almost all of them are aspects of uncertainty.

Every industry differs from all others in the types and relative importance of the risks assumed. Some industries appear to bear unique types of risks. Thus, agriculture and related activities depend uniquely on proper combinations and sequences of sunlight, temperatures, and moisture, and so are uniquely subject to the risks of untimely wind, hail, drought, flood, and freeze. The oil and gas industry also has its unique type of risk: that involved in the search for deposits beneath the surface of the earth. This peculiar type of risk makes the business of finding, developing, and producing crude petroleum and natural gas a candidate for the designation "highly risky."

Risk as a Cost

Before further considering the distinctive risks of the oil and gas industry, it is useful to note some of the economic implications of business risk in general. To the extent that risk is inherent in the natural and institutional environment, it is in effect a cost of producing goods and services of value to man. Differential riskiness among industries tends to be reflected in relative prices and in the allocation of resources among alternative economic pursuits. Risk may be reflected in production costs in one or more of several ways:

(1) It may be reflected in premiums paid for insurance proper (which premiums, in turn, reflect actual losses). (2) It may be reflected in the diseconomies of relatively large investments in liquid, short-lived, and non-specialized assets as a means of maintaining flexibility in planning and weathering possible adversity.[33] (3) It may be reflected in the diseconomies of great size and diversity in the business firm, both used to "pool" risks.[34] (4) It may be reflected simply in the losses on unproductive investments which must be charged against the income from productive investments. And (5), highly important for our purposes, it may be reflected in the high average rate of return required to attract capital into the risky industry.

It is generally assumed (and observation seems to bear this out) that the typical investor in economic undertakings has an "aversion to risk," although the degree of aversion surely varies widely among investors and appears to be negative in many instances.[35] On this assumption, those risks which cannot effectively be dealt with by insurance or by devices of melioration (e.g., high liquidity ratios and diversification) must be reflected in typical rates of return high enough at the margin to overcome, or compensate for, aversion to risk. In effect, the typical investor, faced with a probability distribution of possible returns having great dispersion, withholds his funds from the relatively risky industry until the whole probability distribution is forced up to where the *most probable*, or better the *mathematically expectable*, return is above the *acceptable realized* return—that is, until the chances of the realized rate of return falling below the acceptable rate of return are acceptably small. Other things being the same, then, the average rate of return tends to vary from industry to industry directly with the degree of riskiness. Little dispersion of rates of return by firm may be expected *within* the relatively riskless industries, but great dispersion *within* the relatively risky industries. As a corollary, a substantial difference may be expected between the average rate of return of *successful* firms in the relatively riskless industries and

---

[33] For a full discussion of these devices for meliorating the effects of risk (uncertainty), see Albert G. Hart, *Anticipations, Uncertainty, and Dynamic Planning* (Augustus M. Kelley, 1951), especially pp. 51–74.

[34] There may be compensating economies associated with size and diversification, of course.

[35] Hart, *op. cit.*, pp. 72–74.

the average rate of return of *successful* firms in the relatively risky industries.

Risk in the Oil and Gas Industry

In order to evaluate riskiness in the oil and gas industry, it is useful to identify at least four phases, or functions, in the industry: pre-drilling activities, exploratory drilling, development drilling and equipping of productive wells, and production proper.

PRE-DRILLING ACTIVITIES. These include identifying areas of potential production, acquiring rights to drill in such areas, and locating promising drilling sites. They also include geological and geophysical surveys and the purchase of leases. Depending on the length and intensity of the surveys, the accessibility of the areas under study, and the competition for leases, the outlays involved may be quite substantial.[36] In many instances, between the first

[36] As the following table indicates, geological and geophysical exploration and lease acquisitions (including lease rentals) typically account for over 20 percent of total finding and development costs and about half of total exploration costs.

Industry Expenditure for Finding and Developing Oil
and Gas Deposits 1951, 1953, 1955
(millions of dollars)[a]

	1951	1953	1955	Average % of total
Exploration costs				
Geological, geophysical, and related professional services	186	244	245	5.2
Lease purchases and rentals	638	745	877	17.4
Dry holes	650	796	940	18.4
Overhead	127	171	206	3.9
Total—exploration	1,601	1,995	2,268	44.9
Development costs				
Drilling and completion of producing wells	1,390	1,690	2,097	39.9
Equipment (tubing, tanks, etc.)	420	483	556	11.3
Overhead	136	168	206	3.9
Total—development	1,946	2,341	2,859	55.1
Total exploration and development	3,547	4,296	5,127	100.0

[a] Detail does not always add to totals, due to rounding.

Source: Mid-Continent Oil and Gas Association, *op. cit.*, p. 58, citing C. C. Anderson, *op. cit.*

outlays on exploration in an area and the decision whether to drill or not, several years of testing and lease acquisition pass. Whatever the period of time, the exploratory outlays and lease acquisition costs must be capitalized and accumulated for tax purposes, subject to recovery through depletion if production is later established or to expensing as an ordinary loss if the project is abandoned and the leases surrendered.

EXPLORATORY DRILLING. The second phase, exploratory drilling, is, of course, undertaken to test the hypothesis that oil or gas (or both) is to be found in commercial quantities in a particular area at likely and accessible depths.[37] Such drilling may be quite expensive, again depending upon accessibility, the depth of the test, and the nature of the formations penetrated.[38] If an exploratory well is unsuccessful, its costs may be expensed for tax purposes as an ordinary business loss when the project is abandoned; if it is successful, the intangible costs may be expensed in the current tax period, and the tangible costs must be capitalized subject to recovery through depreciation.

DEVELOPMENT DRILLING. Following a discovery of apparently commercial proportions, the development phase begins. Wells are drilled into the oil- (and/or gas-) bearing formation to gain efficient access to the deposit and incidentally to discover its scope and characteristics. When fully developed, the producing area is covered with producing wells and ringed with dry holes.[39] The former are equipped with the necessary controls, gathering pipes, pumps (if needed) and tanks. Dry hole costs and the intangible and tangible costs of drilling and equipping producing wells are treated for tax purposes as indicated above. These costs, however, being attributable to particular producing properties, may affect the allowable depletion on production from those properties through the 50-percent-of-net limitation.

---

[37] That dry holes are not absolutely conclusive negative indications is evidenced by the many instances on record of companies abandoning interests in an area on the basis of one or more dry holes, only to see others later make discoveries at different sites or depths in the same area. (McKie, *op. cit.*, p. 563.)

[38] See note 36, above.

[39] Of course, dry holes may occur within the general area of production, due to irregularities in the producing formation.

PRODUCTION OF OIL AND GAS. The final phase, production of oil and gas, is self-explanatory. The costs involved, chiefly for labor, repairs, and severance and ad valorem taxes, receive no distinctive treatment for income tax purposes, although they are pertinent to the 50-percent-of-net limitation.

Risk in the Early Phases

The description alone of the four basic phases of activity in the oil and gas industry suggests the risks involved in each. Moreover, it suggests that the degree of risk (more accurately, the degree of uncertainty) tends to diminish from the first to the final phase.

THE PRE-DRILLING PERIOD. In the pre-drilling phase of exploration effort, surface indications of subsurface formations of *a type* known or believed to be *capable* of trapping oil and gas must be relied on. The most modern methods of locating such formations without actually drilling, including use of the seismograph, the gravitymeter, and the magnetometer, are less than perfect, and they cannot indicate with certainty whether oil and gas are present in the typical formations. McKie[40] offers dramatic evidence of uncertainty in the pre-drilling phase by citing the wide variability of lease bonuses bid by major companies for given blocks of acreage in a federal outer continental shelf lease sale of July 1955. In one case, the high bid was fifteen times the low bid. In a half-dozen other cases, the ratios of the high to the low bid ranged from six to ten. In only two of the seven cases cited was the high bidder the same company. Offering further evidence of uncertainty in the pre-drilling phase is the fact that only a modest fraction, perhaps 15 percent, of the costs incurred in this phase ever become attributable to productive properties.[41]

THE EXPLORATORY DRILLING PERIOD. Uncertainty in the drilling phase of exploration is suggested by dry hole statistics. Table 3

[40] *Op. cit.*, pp. 561–62.
[41] As was indicated earlier (note 16), there is evidence that exploration costs attributable to producing properties (hence capitalized and recoverable through cost depletion) amount to about 3 percent of total finding and development costs. There is other evidence (note 36) that total geological, geophysical, and lease acquisition costs are about 20 percent of total finding and development costs. It follows that of the latter about 15 percent are attributable to producing properties ($\frac{3}{20}$ percent). The Mid-Continent Oil and Gas study states without explanation that only 5 percent of such costs are ever attributable to producing properties. (*Op. cit.*, p. 58.)

shows total exploratory wells drilled in the United States in the years 1949 through 1960 and the number and percentage of such wells that were dry. The total is divided into two categories, "new-field wildcats" and "other exploratory wells," the former being wells drilled on formations or in environments never before productive and the latter being wells drilled in a search for new pools or extensions of old ones in formations previously proved productive. The data show that, on the average for the years covered, approximately 90 percent of new-field wildcats were dry, only one in ten resulting in a discovery. The record is naturally somewhat better for other exploratory wells, slightly more than 70 percent of them being dry over the twelve-year period covered. In total, about 80 percent of exploratory wells were dry, which is to say that only one in five resulted in a discovery.

The data suggest that uncertainty is very great for the explorer drilling one or a few wildcat wells. On the other hand, the highly stable ratio of successful wells to total exploratory wells drilled suggests that for major operators who can drill a large number of wildcat wells in a period of several years the degree of success is highly predictable. In other words, the data in Table 3 seem to indicate that the risk associated with wildcat drilling can be "insured" against by drilling a large enough number of wells. Despite its seeming plausibility, this presumption is highly questionable for two reasons: (1) neither the wildcat well nor the discovery is a standardized unit; (2) the universe is not homogeneous, and it is probably not possible for even the largest operators to stratify samples adequately, particularly on a geographical basis.[42] These considerations will be discussed in greater detail below. It is useful first to look at the record of success of some of the largest exploring companies in the United States.

Unfortunately, it is impossible to secure from published sources

---

[42] The economic characteristics of producing areas differ widely on a geographical basis, reflecting differences in depth and size of formations, accessibility, chemical qualities, type of drive, distance to refining centers, and regulatory practices, for instance. Dry hole ratios also differ widely among areas. In 1959 about 38 percent of all wells drilled in the United States (except service wells) were dry. In the same year the dry hole ratio was approximately 70 percent in Colorado, 50 percent or somewhat higher in Illinois, Kansas, Michigan, and Wyoming, and about 22 percent in the Panhandle area of Texas. (American Petroleum Institute, *Petroleum Facts and Figures*, 1961), p. 22.

TABLE 3. Dry Holes in Exploratory Drilling in the United States, by Years, 1949–60

Year	New-field Wildcats[a]			Other Exploratory Wells			Total Exploratory Wells		
	Total	Dry	% Dry	Total	Dry	% Dry	Total	Dry	% Dry
1949	4,448	3,943	88.6	4,610	3,285	71.2	9,058	7,288	79.8
1950	5,290	4,698	88.8	5,016	3,594	71.6	10,306	8,292	80.4
1951	5,189	5,505	88.9	5,567	4,034	72.5	11,756	9,539	81.1
1952	6,698	5,957	88.9	5,727	4,133	72.2	12,425	10,090	81.2
1953	6,925	6,151	88.8	6,388	4,482	70.2	13,313	10,633	79.9
1954	7,380	6,478	87.8	5,717	3,911	68.4	13,097	10,389	79.3
1955	8,104	7,186	88.7	6,833	4,646	68.0	14,937	11,832	79.2
1956	8,709	7,841	90.0	7,464	5,236	70.2	16,173	13,077	80.8
1957	8,014	7,142	89.1	6,693	4,755	71.0	14,707	11,897	80.9
1958	6,950	6,164	88.7	6,249	4,468	71.5	13,199	10,632	80.6
1959	7,031	6,259	89.0	6,160	4,318	70.1	13,191	10,577	80.2
1960	7,320	6,575	89.8	4,384	2,940	67.1	11,704	9,515	81.3
Total	83,058	73,899	89.0	70,808	49,802	70.3	153,866	123,701	80.4

[a] See text for definition.
Source: B. W. Blanpied, "Exploratory Drilling in 1958," *Bulletin of the American Association of Petroleum Geologists* (June 1959), pp. 1124 and 1131; and J. Ben Carsey, "Exploratory Drilling in 1960," *Bulletin of the American Association of Petroleum Geologists* (June 1961), p. 711.

a useful sample of data on exploratory drilling by individual companies. Most companies seem to feel that such information, if published, would hurt their interests. On the other hand, data on total drilling, which are published by a large number of companies, may be adequate for the present purposes. Table 4 shows the total number of wells drilled by eight large companies, the number and percentage of dry holes drilled, and the range of the annual dry hole percentages during the period. These companies together account for about 10 percent of total wells drilled and nearly 30 percent of crude oil production in the United States. It is significant (for reasons that will be indicated later) that each of the eight companies has a much lower average dry hole percentage for the period than do other operators drilling in the United States. But also significant is the wide range of individual company averages. Amerada, one of the more successful purely producing companies in the United States, averaged 29.5 percent dry holes from 1951 through 1960. Phillips, an integrated firm, averaged only 15.4 percent dry holes for the period. The difference could not conceivably be attributed to differences in the number of wells drilled.[43] In addition, for each company, there was a wide range in the percent-

[43] Some of the differences among companies undoubtedly are associated with differences in regional concentration of drilling and in the ratio of exploratory to development drilling. See notes 42 and 44.

Table 4. Dry Holes in Total Drilling of Eight Large Oil Companies, 1951–60

Company	Total Wells Drilled	Dry Holes	Average Percent Dry	Range of Percent Dry by Years, 1951–60
Amerada	3,278	967	29.5	22.5–42.7
Continental	5,194	1,249	24.0	19.6–31.3
Humble	6,736[a]	1,572[a]	23.3[a]	18.1–26.7[a]
Phillips	4,398	679	15.4	11.4–21.0
Shell	9,695	2,094	21.6	16.0–24.6
Sinclair	5,078	1,078	21.2	15.8–28.9
Standard (Calif.)	7,191	1,353	18.8	14.2–25.1
Standard (Ind.)	8,058	1,838	22.8	19.0–29.1
Total drilling in U.S.	464,941	183,009	38.5	36.2–39.9

[a] 1951–57. Recent data merged with those of Standard Oil of New Jersey in source.
Sources: Company data: Standard and Poor's *Corporation Records*. U. S. data: *Oil and Gas Journal*, Annual Review and Outlook issues.

age of dry holes by years. Thus, the range for Amerada in the ten-year period was 22.5 percent to 42.7 percent; for Phillips, 11.4 percent to 21.0 percent. Undoubtedly, some of this range is to be associated with variations in the ratio of exploratory to total drilling by the individual companies,[44] but most of it must be due to the

[44] It is implausible to assume that the observed year-to-year variations by companies are even largely due to changes in the ratio of exploratory to development drilling. In the first place, large companies with continuous drilling programs spread over a great number of active leases in various stages of exploration and development are unlikely to have occasion to alter markedly from year to year the ratio of exploratory to development wells. In the second place, even a doubling of this ratio could not account for the magnitude of the observed variations. To illustrate, assume that in a given year a firm's wells drilled are 20 percent exploratory and 80 percent developmental; that 80 percent of the exploratory wells and 25 percent of the development wells are dry. (These percentages conform approximately to total industry experience in the past decade. See Table 3 and notes 42 and 46.) The firm's average proportion of dry holes in that year would be 36 percent. Now suppose that in the following year the same percentage of dry holes is experienced in each category, but that the firm doubles its percentage of exploratory wells. The ratios then are 40 percent exploratory and 60 percent developmental. The average experience of the firm becomes 47 percent dry holes, something less than a third larger than that of the previous year. Now let the firm have a dry hole experience that is exactly one-half that of the industry, so that only 40 percent of its exploratory wells are dry and $12\frac{1}{2}$ percent of its developmental wells are dry. With 20 percent of its wells exploratory, it will average 18 percent dry holes (a figure more in keeping with the averages in Table 4). Doubling the exploratory percentage now increases the average dry hole ratio to 23.5 percent, again a gain of something less than a third. The typical relative difference in Table 4 is close to twice that figure.

simple unpredictability of drilling results when even a relatively large number of wells are drilled.

The foregoing data suggest that simple probability models cannot be used to predict with accuracy even so crude a measure of success in drilling as the percentage of "hits" to "tries." The *economic* evaluation of risk in drilling, hence the problem of predicting *economic* success, is still more complex. Consider first that a well drilled in search for new deposits of oil or gas is not a uniform economic unit. It may be deep or shallow, drilled in accessible or inaccessible places through formations difficult or easy to penetrate. It may have behind it merely a hunch and a small lease or months and years of surface testing and a huge investment in a lease block. In short, it may be a cheap or an expensive hole in the ground, and the expense is not fully measured by the cost of drilling proper.

On the other side of the economic equation is the fact that a "hit" is not a uniform economic unit. Discoveries vary widely in their size, chemical qualities, producing characteristics, and economic location. Moreover, a finder's benefits from his own discovery depend on his proportionate holding of surface rights in the area that turns out to be productive, and even on the location of his holdings within the productive area. The data in Table 5 show recent variations in the size of discoveries of crude oil. Discoveries are rated after several years (seven and four in the present case) of experience in development and production, since the size of recoverable reserves in a deposit cannot be determined with certainty immediately upon discovery. (This fact is of obvious relevance to the risks involved in development, to be discussed below.) Table 5 indicates that the odds on discoveries get progressively smaller as the size of the reserves increases. The odds on fields of 25 million barrels or more are extremely small. Yet the fact that the larger discoveries have been made in the past undoubtedly makes exploratory activity attractive and at the same time makes uncertain the outcome of even a relatively large number of wells drilled in a year.

There is a rule of thumb in the industry that a field must ordinarily contain one million barrels or more of recoverable reserves to be profitable in the sense of yielding a satisfactory return on all costs, including attributable exploration costs. (Of course, it is profitable to develop and produce a field, once discovered, if

Table 5. Oil Fields Discovered in 1954 and 1957 in the United States, by Ultimate Reserves, Estimated as of January 1, 1961
(Seventeen-state area[a])

Reserve Group (in millions of barrels)	Year of Discovery	
	1954	1957
	(number of fields)	
A 50 or more	2	0
B 25 but less than 50	3	2
C 10 but less than 25	13	19
D 1 but less than 10	99	73
E Less than 1 but not abandoned	369	574
F Abandoned	188	126
Total classes A and B	5	2
Total classes C and D	112	92
Total all classes	674	794

[a] Includes Alabama, Arkansas, California, Colorado, Illinois, Indiana, Kansas, Kentucky, Louisiana, Michigan, Mississippi, Montana, Nebraska, New Mexico, Oklahoma, Texas, and Wyoming.
Source: Carsey, op. cit. p. 714.

it yields no more than a satisfactory return on development costs.) Table 6 throws some light on the chances of discovering fields of one million barrels of reserves or more. Not only are the chances small; they are relatively quite variable, the highest success ratio in the period being 165 percent of the lowest. Year-to-year variations of 50 percent or more in the ratios are observable. Because the category "one million barrels or more" is extremely broad, these data suggest that, for reasons of deposit size alone, economic success in even sizable wildcat programs may be highly unpredictable. In addition, it should be re-emphasized that discovery of a field of given size is not tantamount to having secured the full worth of that field for the discoverer's benefit. A large interest in a small field may be worth more than a small interest in a large field. The full meaning of success in exploratory drilling must be derived from the proportionate ownership (lessee interest) of the explorer in whatever is discovered.

The data in Tables 5 and 6 pertain to oil field and recoverable crude oil reserves. Also pertinent to any economic evaluation of success in drilling are discoveries of gas, either separate from, or in association with, petroleum. Unhappily there seems to be no

Table 6. Success Ratios After Six Years of Development, New Field
Wildcats, 1944–54
(Seventeen-state area^a)

Year of Drilling or Discovery	Total New-Field Wildcats Drilled[b]	Percent of Total Successful	Percent Resulting in Fields of 1 Million Barrels or More
1944	3,014	11.0	2.8
1945	2,913	11.5	2.4
1946	2,995	10.4	2.4
1947	3,325	11.4	2.3
1948	4,087	11.5	2.3
1949	4,238	11.4	2.6
1950	5,149	11.2	2.4
1951	6,044	11.0	2.1
1952	6,440	11.2	1.8
1953	6,634	11.3	2.4
1954	7,033	12.4	1.7

^a See note to Table 5.
^b These totals differ from those in Table 3, due to reclassifications after discovery.
Source: Carsey, op. cit. p. 715.

thoroughly satisfactory way of combining gas results with crude oil results, partly because of the relative valuation problem and partly because the economic significance of associated gas may for many years following discovery be derived from the use of such gas to help expel crude oil from the bearing formation. Put in another way, gas in association with crude oil is a determinant of the economic value of the crude oil; if such gas is retained for a while as a cap, or is recycled, it has no value for such a period separate from that of the oil. For this reason known oil and gas reserves cannot simply be separately evaluated and the values summed to a meaningful total. In the case of nonassociated gas, on the other hand, the separate values discovered are highly pertinent to an evaluation of exploration results.

Table 7 shows the distribution by reserve size of gas fields discovered in 1953 and 1954. At a conversion ratio of one barrel of crude oil to six thousand cubic feet of natural gas, based on relative BTU content,[45] the reserve size classification in Table 7 is

[45] The economically relevant conversion ratio is that expressed in terms of typical relative discounted values of newly discovered reserves in the ground. Data pertinent to such a ratio are not known to the author. In any case, the ratio would change over time, due principally to changing relative prices of oil and gas at the well head.

comparable to that of Table 5, pertaining to reserves of crude oil discovered. On the basis of gas discoveries in 1953 and 1954, it appears that the distribution of reserve sizes in gas fields is less skewed than the corresponding distribution of reserve sizes in oil fields. Nonetheless, the patterns are similar, with the chances of large discoveries being slight for both.

Since the reserve classes used for oil and gas field tabulations are comparable at the six-to-one BTU content ratio, the oil and gas field discovery data may be combined into one table. Carsey has made a combined tabulation for the period 1943–54, the results of which are presented in Table 8 below. But it should be remembered that the BTU content conversion ratio is not necessarily valid for economic purposes. At different relative values of oil and gas reserves, the discovery pattern indicated by Table 8 would mean different probabilities of economic success. Indeed, it is important to point out that uncertainty as to the future relation of oil and gas values contributes to uncertainty in the exploratory phase of the oil and gas industry.

If the exploratory well, including the pre-drilling investment behind it, were a uniform economic unit, *if* oil and gas fields were uniform as to chemical qualities of reserves, operating character-

Table 7. Gas Fields Discovered in 1953 and 1954 in the United States, by Ultimate Reserves, Estimated as of January 1, 1961
(Seventeen-state area[a])

Reserve Group (in billions of cubic feet)	Year of Discovery	
	1953	1954
	(number of fields)	
A 300 or more	7	3
B 150 but less than 300	5	2
C 60 but less than 150	9	10
D 6 but less than 60	41	51
E Less than 6 but not abandoned	89	112
F Abandoned	20	39
Total classes A and B	12	5
Total classes C and D	50	61
Total all classes	171	217

[a] See note to Table 5.
Source: Carsey, op. cit., p. 722.

TABLE 8. Total Oil and Gas Fields Discovered in 1943–54 in the United States, by Reserve Class, Estimated as of January 1, 1961
(*Seventeen-state area*[a])

Reserve class[b]	Number of Fields Discovered 1943–54
A	102
B	101
C	260
D	1,273
E	3,307
F	1,195
Total classes A and B	203
Total classes C and D	1,533
Total all classes	6,238

[a] See note to Table 5.
[b] See description of classes, Tables 5 and 7.
Source: Carsey, op. cit., p. 725.

istics, and economic location, *if* the gas-oil price ratio were constant, and *if* the universe of discoverable fields were homogeneous with respect to different explorers, the exploration for oil and gas might be reduced to a problem in probabilities, and any firm could effectively insure results by drilling a large enough number of wells. With respect to the last "if," most firms, because of historical origins, legal restraints, location of refinery and marketing facilities, managerial biases, and the like, tend to devote most of their exploration efforts to a few geographical areas in the United States (and the world). In addition, the economics and administrative problems of pre-drilling work—especially the intensive and continuing study of geological and geophysical data, and the amassing of suitable lease blocks—probably make it unfeasible for even the very largest companies literally to blanket the country (and the world) with exploratory effort. Some regional specialization is probably essential to satisfactory pre-drilling work. The result is that each company in effect operates in a different probability universe from every other company. The experience of other companies and of all explorers taken together is thus a highly imperfect indication of probable success in exploration by any one company.

The mere listing of "if's" in the preceding paragraph is enough to show that exploring for oil and gas is not an exercise in known probabilities, but means investing in the face of considerable uncertainty.

Risk in the Later Phases

HAZARDS OF THE DEVELOPMENT PERIOD. Turning now to the third phase of the industry, the development of discoveries, one can readily see that the risks here are smaller than those in the exploratory phase. The presence of oil or gas of given chemical qualities is known. There remains only the task of determining, through further drilling and production, the extent and operating characteristics of the deposit discovered. Yet development too has its hazards, as non-exploratory dry hole statistics show. In the ten-year period 1951–60, approximately 25 percent of all development wells (exclusive of service wells) were dry.[46] To some extent, development dry holes are predictable, and their probable costs can be taken into account in making the development decision; for when a producing area is finally delimited, it must be ringed with dry holes. However, they are not necessarily *highly* predictable, because the proportion of dry holes to producing wells ultimately depends on the size of the producing area and its irregularities, neither of which can be determined in advance. There is the further problem in development of discovering the exact nature and efficiency of the expulsion mechanism, or "drive," which goes far to determine production costs and ultimately recoverable reserves.

GENERAL RISKS OF THE PRODUCTION PERIOD. In the final phase of the industry—production, which overlaps development in some measure—the risks are about the same as those faced by any other business. They pertain to costs, prices, general business fluctuations, obsolescence, taxation, regulation, and the like. In some respects, the oil or gas producer *per se* faces fewer or less severe hazards than his counterparts in other industries. The price elasticity of demand for his product is quite low: certainly less than unity. Regulation of production under "market demand" conservation statutes in the case of oil results in relatively stable and predictable prices. Gas prices are made similarly stable and predictable in many instances by long-term contracts with pipelines and distributors. Sudden

[46] *Oil and Gas Journal*, Annual Review and Outlook issues.

obsolescence seems not to be a problem in the industry, although the probability and imminence of severe competition from alternative sources of energy are now increasing with each passing year. The sensitivity of demand for oil and gas to general business fluctuations is probably less than that for most mineral products. On the other hand, it must be noted that both the price elasticity of demand for oil and gas and the sensitivity of demand for these products to business fluctuations have shown signs of increasing in recent years as oil products, gas, and coal have become closer substitutes at prevailing price relationships. Regulation of oil production, while tending to stabilize prices, introduces risks concerning rates of production and unit costs. Regulation of gas prices, particularly recently, must be regarded as a source of uncertainty in the calculations of explorers and producers. But all things considered, despite the impossibility of making direct comparisons of risk "packages," it seems safe to say that oil and gas production *per se* is among neither the most nor the least risky of modern industries, and that it is probably less risky than other phases of the oil and gas industry as a whole.

The four-phase classification of risks in the industry is useful because it provides a means of classifying firms in the industry on the basis of functions performed and risks assumed. Some firms—all of the integrated companies and most of the principal unaffiliated producing companies—engage in all phases of the industry, from pre-drilling work to production proper. Others engage in one, two, or three of the phases. For instance, there are consulting geologists, firms specializing in geophysical services, contract drillers, and operators of producing properties that were purchased after extensive or complete development. There are explorer-producers who rely exclusively on specialists for pre-drilling exploration. There are drilling contractors who operate exclusively on a fee basis, and there are others who assume some of the costs of drilling in exchange for a share in what is discovered. There are still other independent entrepreneur-drillers who finance exploratory wells by securing contributions to drilling costs from companies interested in the results of a test in a particular area. The sum of such contributions often exceeds the cost of the wells financed, but the driller retains for himself a share in any discoveries made.[47] In short, the structure

---

[47] See McKie, *op. cit.*, pp. 566–69, for a detailed explanation of the operations of such entrepreneurs.

of the industry is such that a firm may engage in selected phases of it, and in any given phase assume great or slight risks as it chooses. This is another reason why the dry hole, for instance, is not a significant unit in appraising the economic risks in the industry; why the search for oil and gas is not a game of chance, the odds on success being revealed in tables of historical dry hole ratios.[48]

An important aspect of risk selection in the industry relates to pre-drilling exploration work. The large, integrated companies—often called "majors"—typically have a higher percentage of successful wildcat wells than do the "independents" or "minors."[49] Some, if not all, of this difference may be attributed to greater preparatory effort by the "majors" in the form of geological and geophysical testing,[50] which, inconclusive though it is, tends to reduce uncertainty. The "independents," with relatively restricted financial resources, tend to "explore with the bit" and to confine wildcatting to comparatively shallow and otherwise inexpensive wells. The "majors" are more disposed to make the relatively expensive tests at extreme depths and in unusual or inaccessible places, but only after careful, often lengthy, pre-drilling exploration.[51] There are, in effect, many "games" that an operator can play under the general heading of wildcat drilling. Each "game" has its own cost per "try" and probability of success per "try." And the probability of success varies directly with the cost per "try." Accordingly, an operator may select an optimum "game" in the light of his financial resources and attitude toward risk taking.

Measures of Relative Risk

To cite the hazards in the oil and gas industry does no more than establish that there is some objective basis of risk—or, more properly, of uncertainty—in the industry. There is no satisfactory way to compare different risk "packages" among industries and to conclude that one industry is "highly" risky or more risky than another. For comparative purposes, one must rely on indirect evidence of riskiness. Unfortunately, such evidence is scanty indeed

[48] This is also why it is impossible to generalize about risks assumed on the basis of company size.
[49] McKie, *op. cit.*, p. 550.
[50] *Ibid.*, p. 551.
[51] *Ibid.*, pp. 551–52.

in the oil and gas industry. It would be most helpful to be able to compare mortality or turnover rates for particular classes of firms within the industry with such rates in other industries. To the author's knowledge, no such comparative studies covering the oil and gas industry have been made.[52] One would be inclined to associate relative riskiness with relative instability of income and marked changes in market shares over time. However, the value of such a comparison is questionable in the case of the oil and gas industry. Current income, as reported by conventional accounting methods in the industry, reflects production from existing reserves (which, as noted, is subject to relatively few hazards) and current *expenditure* on exploration and development. Because large reserve inventories are usual in oil and gas production, current income as reported is not sensitive to current success in exploration and development.[53] Changes in market shares over time do not necessarily indicate the degree of success in exploration and development because proven properties are bought and sold easily and frequently. Comparative data on changes in reserves by various companies through their exploration and development efforts would help reveal the objective basis of risk in the industry. But such data would not be released by many firms, if any; and, in any case, they would not provide a valid basis for comparing the risks in the oil and gas industry with those in other industries.

Degree of riskiness is often associated with credit rationing, the relatively risky industries having to rely heavily on equity funds. Debt-equity ratios might in some cases provide an indication of relative riskiness among industries. But in the case of the oil and gas industry, a valid comparison cannot be made on the basis of debt-equity ratios because statistics are not available that segregate the purely producing phase from the exploration and development phases. It is quite easy to borrow on the basis of proven reserves because of relative price stability, divisibility of ownership in oil and gas, and separability of oil and gas from other assets. An explorer with some past record of success may borrow on his proven reserves in order to finance further exploration effort, often pledging

---

[52] An inquiry about the possible existence of such studies addressed to the U. S. Department of Commerce received a negative reply.

[53] A relatively small company making a relatively large discovery might provide a significant exception to this generalization.

specific portions of each period's production from proven reserves to payment of interest and reduction of principal.[54] The lender in effect finances exploration, but the lender's risks are in no way associated with the success of the exploration effort financed. The volume of debt in the oil and gas industry reflects chiefly the risks in the purely producing phase only.

Since risk is essentially a subjective matter, the ultimate test of relative riskiness is the valuation investors put on the prospective income streams to which they acquire claims. As noted earlier, relative riskiness is associated with relatively high rates of return, assuming that the typical investor has an aversion to risk. Consequently, perhaps the best single evidence of comparative riskiness in the oil and gas industry would be a relatively high average rate of return over a long period, or over a shorter period that may reasonably be regarded as "normal," particularly if restriction of entry is not a factor.

Unfortunately, because of three important characteristics of the petroleum industry data, an adequate comparison is impossible. First, due to the industry's internal accounting practice of expensing dry hole and other unsuccessful exploration costs (and, in the case of some companies, of intangible development costs also),[55] accounting statements do not necessarily show exactly the economic results of current operations. Net assets tend to be understated because the full value of oil and gas discovered is not reflected in the investment outlays that are capitalized. For similar reasons, the current net income of the industry tends also to be understated. The two understatements are not necessarily offsetting, however, since the former reflects the cumulative results of the past while the latter reflects current results of operations. Moreover, to an unknown extent the tendency to understate net assets is "corrected" in the aggregate of accounting records in the industry by sales of proven properties, the sales prices being capitalized in the purchasing companies' books. How much all these effects cause reported and actual rates of return to diverge, it is impossible to say on the basis of currently available evidence.

Second, it appears that about two-thirds of the oil and gas

---

[54] For an explanation of borrowing on the collateral of a "production payment," see Charles O. Galvin in *Harvard Law Review* (June 1960), pp. 1500–02.

[55] See pp. 22–23 above.

production at home and abroad by American companies is by firms for which oil and gas production is not the largest single source of receipts.[56] These firms engage in one or more other activities, such as refining, transportation, or marketing, and their reported rates of return reflect in large part current results from these activities. There is no way of determining from published reports what are the rates of return of these firms on the allegedly more risky activity of finding, developing, and producing oil and gas. And there is no certainty that the rates of return reported by the other companies—those whose activities are confined more narrowly to finding, developing, and producing oil and gas, but which account for only about one-third of the total production of American companies—are representative of the industry as a whole.

Third, most of the major integrated companies and many of the specialized producing companies domiciled in this country derive substantial amounts of oil and gas production income from foreign operations. Several of the largest integrated concerns have a larger volume of production abroad than at home.[57] Domestic conditions under which oil and gas are found and produced differ from those abroad in many ways. Circumstances of natural occurrence, systems of regulation, other political restraints, and freedom of competitive entry are often markedly different. Rates of return that reflect a combination of foreign and domestic production, therefore, may be indicative of factors other than risk. If risk alone is a factor, it may be a composite risk that is not necessarily comparable with that assumed by other industries operating almost exclusively at home.

For these reasons, a discussion of available data on comparative rates of return would inevitably be inconclusive. However, some

[56] In its compilations of data derived from corporation income tax returns, the Internal Revenue Service classifies corporations according to the largest single source of receipts. Oil and gas production is reflected in at least two major industrial classifications, "Petroleum and Coal Products" in the general category of "Manufacturing," and "Crude Petroleum and Natural Gas" in the general category of "Mining." The depletion deductions of corporations in the former classification have been in recent years about two-thirds of the total for both classifications, suggesting a similar division of oil and gas production. (U. S. Treasury Department, Internal Revenue Service, *Statistics of Income, Part 2, Corporation Income Tax Returns.*)

[57] For instance, Standard Oil Co. (New Jersey), Texaco, Socony Mobil Oil Co., Gulf Oil Corp., and Standard Oil Co. of California.

widely used data, together with some comments on their limitations and possible significance, are presented in Appendix A.

Risk and the Distinctive Tax Provisions

Assuming for the sake of argument that the industry is in fact a relatively risky one, what bearing does this have on the present distinctive tax provisions that have the effect of taxing income from oil and gas production at a lower rate than income from most other sources? The economist's instinctive first reaction is that relative riskiness does not justify differentially low taxation. After all, risk is simply another cost of production, and an optimum allocation of resources requires, among other things, that all prices fully reflect underlying costs. On the other hand, however, under certain assumptions a case can be made for the view that income taxation at uniform rates places greater cost burdens on relatively risky industries. This suggests that lower income tax rates for the more risky industries may be consistent with an optimum allocation of productive resources.

To clarify the issues, it is helpful to begin with the standard economic criticism of the distinctive tax provisions, which have the effect of lowering effective tax rates on income derived from the production of oil, gas, and other affected minerals. For purposes of the model used in presenting the criticism[58] abstract from all taxes except the corporate income tax, which for all practical purposes may be regarded as a flat-rate tax. Ignore also differences in risk among industries, and so assume that investors discount expected streams of income at the same rates. Assume that the corporate income tax is not shifted and that its full burden rests both initially and ultimately on the suppliers of capital, reducing rates of return in proportion to the tax.

THE HARBERGER MODEL. To illustrate the effects on allocation of resources of differential taxation under these assumptions, imagine two kinds of assets (corresponding to two different industries), one

[58] The model is that of Arnold C. Harberger as presented in "The Taxation of Mineral Industries," *Federal Tax Policy for Economic Growth and Stability*, a compendium of papers presented to the Joint Committee on the Economic Report, 84 Cong. 1 sess. (1955), pp. 439–49. See especially pp. 447–49.

a machine and the other a mineral deposit. Assume that these two assets are equivalent in the sense that the streams of income expected from them, net of other costs, but before provision for depreciation or depletion, are identical. It is readily apparent that these two assets would be equally attractive to investors if (a) there were no income tax or if (b) the two income streams were subject to identical effective rates of taxation (implying like schedules of depreciation and depletion). Hence, with equal effective rates of taxation, the allocation of capital between the two kinds of assets (two different industries) would be the same as if there were no tax at all.[59] But, if income from the mineral deposit were subjected to a lower effective tax than income from the machine because of accelerated deduction of costs and a special deduction in addition to costs actually incurred, its present worth would become greater than that of the machine under a nominally uniform income tax.[60] Capital would flow from machines to mineral deposits. Products of machines would become less plentiful and their prices would tend to rise. Products of mineral deposits would become more plentiful, and their prices would tend to fall. Eventually a new equilibrium would be achieved in which machines and mineral deposits were equally attractive, but in this equilibrium there would be a larger output of mineral products at lower prices and a smaller output of the product of machines at higher prices than in the absence of an income tax or with equal rates of income tax.

In effect, the differential income taxation subsidizes the production and consumption of mineral products at the expense of the production and consumption of the products of machines. Since there has been no shift in either relative demands or relative real costs of production, the shift in relative outputs represents a misallocation of resources that must lead to smaller aggregate real satisfactions than otherwise would have resulted from the total resources used. In short, the differential taxation imposes a net real cost on society as a whole. To avoid such a cost, taxation must be

[59] It may be noted in passing that this conclusion abstracts from any income effect of the tax upon relative demands, and from any shift in relative demands resulting from government expenditure of the tax proceeds.

[60] An adaptation of Harberger's algebraic model, which demonstrates this point, is given in Appendix B.

"neutral" with respect to the allocation of resources among alternative uses; and "neutral" taxation, it follows from the foregoing model, requires that equal effective rates be applied to all forms of return to capital in all alternative uses.[61]

The key assumption in the foregoing model is that the income tax in question is in no part shifted, the full burden of it falling on the suppliers of capital and reducing realized rates of return in proportion to the tax. (This assumption implies that the supply of capital is perfectly inelastic with respect to both the rate of return on capital and the disposable income of capitalists.[62]) On this assumption, the effects of differential taxation are to induce a redistribution of resources among alternative uses and to change the relative prices of different kinds of output. If one assumes that the tax is shifted, wholly or in part, another kind of effect is involved: the money price of final products must rise relative to the money price of land and labor taken together. The adjustment required is larger for

---

[61] In a later paper dealing with the general effects of the corporation income tax in the United States, Harberger makes it clear that to be neutral under his assumptions, a flat-rate income tax would have to fall equally on all forms of return to capital in all uses, and not just on the net income of the corporate sector. In the same paper he explicitly recognizes that the issue of tax neutrality is one that must be approached in terms of the entire tax system, of which, in the United States, the corporation income tax is only a major part. (Arnold C. Harberger, "The Corporation Income Tax: An Empirical Appraisal," *Tax Revision Compendium*, Vol. 1, papers submitted to the Committee on Ways and Means of the House of Representatives, U. S. Congress, Committee Print [November 1959], pp. 231–32 and 235.)

[62] In support of the argument that the corporation income tax is not shifted, it is not enough to observe that saving seems to be inelastic with respect to the rate of interest. Even if "the rate of interest" is taken to be synonymous with the rate of return on capital, this observation seems to confuse the propensity to save out of a given level of disposable income with the supply of resources available for capital formation. A tax on the income of capitalists must at least initially reduce their disposable income. Thus, even if saving is totally inelastic with respect to the rate of return on capital and is a simple function of private disposable income, the supply of resources available for capital formation is reduced by the tax.

In a recent article on the incidence of the corporation income tax, Harberger notes the income effect of the tax on the supply of saving but, for the purposes at hand, disregards it because any other tax yielding similar revenues would have similar income effects. This procedure is consistent with Harberger's definition of incidence in a comparative rather than an absolute sense. (Arnold C. Harberger, "The Incidence of the Corporation Income Tax," *Journal of Political Economy*, Vol. 70 [June 1962], p. 216.) The procedure does not seem to the present writer to be valid in analyzing the burden of a tax imposed where none existed before.

those industries in which the return to capital is a relatively large proportion of total factor costs. If, under the assumption that the tax is shifted, such industries are accorded differentially low tax rates, it is not necessarily true that a misallocation of resources will result.

THE MCDONALD MODEL. So as to make the explanatory model[63] and its results as comparable as possible with those of the foregoing Harberger model, the same simplifying assumptions are made (a two-industry economy, each industry subject only to a flat-rate corporation income tax), and it is assumed that the tax is shifted forward in the form of increased money prices of final output. Under the latter assumption, implying permissive monetary conditions, any changes in the relative prices of final goods that may take place are more clearly revealed. The basic difference in the models is that we regard risk (used here to embrace uncertainty) as a genuine cost of production, so that risk assumption must be compensated to call forth investment. It is further assumed then that the taxation of income from capital discourages investment. Thus, for the same amount of investment to occur in the long run, given the industry composition of investment, a tax on the return to capital must be shifted in the sense that after-tax rates of return must be restored to pre-tax levels.[64] One way of restoring after-tax

[63] The following exposition is based on Stephen L. McDonald, "Percentage Depletion and the Allocation of Resources: The Case of Oil and Gas," *National Tax Journal*, Vol. 14 (December 1961), pp. 329–36. The argument relies heavily on analyses of the incidence and effects of the corporation income tax by Carl S. Shoup, "Incidence of the Corporation Income Tax: Capital Structure and Turnover Rates," *National Tax Journal*, Vol. 1 (March 1948), reprinted in American Economic Association, *Readings in the Economics of Taxation*, Vol. 9 (Richard D. Irwin, 1959), pp. 322–29, and J. Fred Weston, "Incidence and Effects of the Corporate Income Tax," *National Tax Journal*, Vol. 2 (December 1949), pp. 313–14. For critical comment on the McDonald article, see Richard A. Musgrave, "Another Look at Depletion," and Douglas H. Eldridge, "Rate of Return, Resource Allocation and Percentage Depletion," both in *National Tax Journal*, Vol. 15 (June 1962), pp. 205–08 and 209–17; and Stephen L. McDonald, "Percentage Depletion and Tax Neutrality: A Reply to Messrs. Musgrave and Eldridge," *National Tax Journal*, Vol. 15 (September 1962), pp. 314–26.

[64] There is a growing body of literature supporting the argument that, because a minimum return on capital is a long-run cost, the corporation income tax tends to be shifted, in the sense used here, in the long run. For a review of this literature, see B. U. Ratchford and P. B. Han, "The Burden of the Corporate Income Tax," *National Tax Journal*, Vol. 10 (December 1957). (Additional references may be found in McDonald, *op. cit.*, p. 329.) Of particular interest is an article by Eugene M. Lerner and Eldon S. Hendriksen ("Federal Taxes on Corporate Income and the Rate of Return on Invest-

rates of return to pre-tax levels is to reduce the input of capital relative to output by substituting labor for capital; but still with a view to focusing all reallocative effects of the tax on changes in relative prices of final goods, it is assumed here that the ratio of capital to output remains constant.[65] Forward shifting in the present sense therefore means preservation of capital's *share* of private disposable income, the owners of capital bearing the real burden of the tax in proportion to that share.[66] It does not mean that the owners of capital bear none of the real burden.

To demonstrate the price effect of a flat-rate corporation income tax under the above assumptions, let all money values be expressed as amounts per unit of product. Let n represent the ratio of the return on capital (N) to sales price (P) in the initial situation of no tax.[67] Then:

$$(1) \qquad n = \frac{r}{v},$$

---

ment in Manufacturing, 1927 to 1952," *National Tax Journal*, Vol. 9 [September 1956]), which gives rather convincing empirical evidence of shifting in the present sense by showing the long-run constancy of rates of return on investment in manufacturing under widely different rates of taxation.

Economists are by no means agreed on the matter, however. Empirical data are subject to different interpretations, and the premises of logical arguments are acceptable in unequal degrees among students of tax incidence. In perhaps the most thorough study of the corporation income tax in the postwar period, Richard Goode (*The Corporation Income Tax* [John Wiley & Sons, 1951], especially pp. 44–62 and 111–47) found little basis for accepting the full shifting argument. An excellent review of the opposing views on the incidence of the corporation income tax, and of the pertinent empirical evidence, is given in John F. Due, *Government Finance: An Economic Analysis* (rev. ed., Richard D. Irwin, 1959), pp. 223–31. Due finds the weight of argument in favor of the view that the tax is shifted in the long run.

[65] See below for further discussion of this assumption.

[66] By assumption, in the long run money wages, the rate of return on capital, and the ratio of capital used to output (the latter measured net of tax-induced price changes) remain constant. Hence the *nominal* (undeflated) amounts of, and the ratio between, labor income and capital income remain constant. But since the postulated tax-induced price changes reduce the *real* incomes of laborers and capitalists in proportion to their money incomes, abstracting from differences in expenditure patterns, the real burden of the tax falls on laborers and capitalists in proportion to their initial money incomes and relative shares.

[67] This ratio is also the ratio of the return on capital to value added when there are no inputs other than direct factor inputs purchased by the economic unit in question. In the following discussion, two mutually independent industries are hypothesized. By hypothesis, then, the sales price of the product of each industry is the value added per unit of product of that industry.

where r = rate of return on capital (N/K) in the initial situation and v = turnover of capital (P/K) in the initial situation. Assume that r is the normal equilibrium value that will be restored through price adjustment to a corporation income tax when imposed, and that v is a constant throughout the adjustment process. Let n' be defined as N'/P, where N' is the return on capital gross of tax after full adjustment to the tax (T). By definition, T = tN', where t is the effective income tax rate. Full incorporation of the tax into the sales price requires that:

$$(2) \qquad\qquad P' = P + tN',$$

where P' is the sales price after full adjustment to the tax. The percentage change in price on account of the tax (p) is:

$$(3) \qquad\qquad \frac{P' - P}{P} = \frac{tN'}{P} = tn'.$$

By definition:

$$n' - tn' = n$$

$$n' = \frac{n}{1 - t}$$

$$(4) \qquad\qquad tn' = \frac{tn}{1 - t} \, .$$

Substituting from equations (1) and (3) in (4), we have:

$$(5) \qquad\qquad p = \frac{t(r/v)}{1 - t} \, .$$

It can be seen, then, that the percentage increase in price resulting from incorporation of the income tax into the price is a positive function of the rate of tax and the equilibrium rate of return, and a negative function of the rate of capital turnover. Given the tax rate, the higher the equilibrium rate of return and the lower the rate of capital turnover, the greater is the percentage increase in price. Risk, it has been argued, is reflected in the rate of return. Given the rate of capital turnover, therefore, the greater the degree of risk, the greater is the percentage change in price as a result of the tax.[68]

[68] An adaptation of the basic Harberger model to show the relative price effects of differential risk and differential capital turnover is presented in Appendix C.

Applying the above generalizations to the comparison of two different industries—manufacturing (1) and minerals production (2), as in the Harberger model—it can be seen that if the same effective tax rate is applied to the two, they will experience the same percentage change in price only if $(r/v)_1 = (r/v)_2$. If $(r/v)_2$ is larger than $(r/v)_1$, then equal effective rates of taxation will mean a rise in the relative price of the product of industry (2) and a reallocation of resources at the expense of that industry. In this case, as in any other involving unequal (r/v) ratios, equal effective rates of taxation are not neutral.

Of course, neutrality could be achieved by making appropriate adjustments in relative effective tax rates. One way of doing this, which is patterned after existing procedures in American mineral industries, is to allow the industry with the higher (r/v) ratio a special exclusion from its gross income. Let d represent this exclusion expressed as a percentage of the initial price P. The condition of neutrality is that:

$$d = (r/v)_2 - (r/v)_1.[69]$$

If the exclusion is expressed as a percentage of the adjusted price P', then the exclusion so expressed (e) is equal to $d/(1 + p_1)$, where p_1 is the percentage increase in the price of the product of industry (1). Accordingly,

$$(6) \qquad e = \frac{(r/v)_2 - (r/v)_1}{1 + p_1}.$$

Unfortunately, data satisfactory for computing a neutralizing value of "e" for oil and gas production are not available. For reasons given earlier, rates of return in the oil and gas industry shown by accounting statements may not accurately reflect economically realized or expected rates of return to the investor. One cannot be sure, moreover, that realized rates of return are unaffected by distinctive tax treatment. Reported capital turnover rates in the industry probably are more reliable, but they may be artificially

[69] See equation (4) above. The derivation of that equation shows that n is the ratio of net income after taxes to the base price (P). Equation (4) shows that if $n_2 = n_1$ per tax return, then the percentage increase in price is the same for each industry. The tax-return equality requires that $(N/P)_1 = (N/P)_2 - (D/P)$, which reduces to $d = n_2 - n_1$. Since $n = (r/v)$, then $d = (r/v)_2 - (r/v)_1$.

lowered by excessive drilling and other inefficiencies induced by state regulation in combination with distinctive tax treatment. (See Chapter V.) Finally, no sample of industry records is available from which to derive rate of return and capital turnover data for the finding-production phase of the industry, properly weighted for foreign and domestic production and free of influences from refining, transportation, marketing, and other activities which do not receive distinctive tax treatment.[70] Perhaps the best that can be done here is to indicate the values of "e" corresponding to different

TABLE 9. Indicated Values of "e" as a Percentage of Gross Income Corresponding to Different Rates of Return and Capital Turnover in the Oil and Gas Industry[a]

Annual Turnover of Stockholders' Equity	Rate of Return on Stockholders' Equity			
	10%	15%	20%	25%
.90	5.6	10.9	16.2	21.5
.85	6.3	11.8	17.4	23.0
.80	6.9	12.9	18.8	24.8
.75	7.7	14.1	20.4	26.7

[a] Assumes a rate of return of 12 percent and annual capital turnover of 2.3 for manufacturing, and an effective tax rate on taxable income of 50 percent.

combinations of rate of return and capital turnover in the finding-production phase of the industry. From such values of "e" one can observe the combinations of rate of return and capital turnover that would be required to support the present extent of distinctive tax treatment, the net effective benefits of which are estimated to be the equivalent of an "e" of approximately 22 percent.[71]

The values of "e" presented in Table 9 are computed from rates of return and capital turnover based on stockholders' equity, after-tax returns to stockholders, and gross income adjusted for income taxes paid. Trial calculations indicate that no significant changes would result from basing computations on total capital employed, after-tax income on total capital employed, and gross income adjusted for income taxes paid and imputed to total returns on capital. For manufacturing, the industry taken as the standard

[70] See Appendix A for a discussion of some data on comparative rates of return and their defects.
[71] See notes 16 and 21.

of comparison, the rate of return used is 12 percent, and capital turnover 2.3 times per year, these being the average values for all manufacturing corporations (except those in the petroleum and coal products category) in the United States reporting net income and filing balance sheets with income tax returns in the years 1949–51 and 1953–56, inclusive.[72] It is assumed that the average effective tax rate on taxable income is 50 percent.

The rate of return and capital turnover that are representative of the finding-production phase of the oil and gas industry probably are within the ranges covered by Table 9.[73] But the indicated value of "e" varies from 5.6 percent to 26.7 percent within those ranges. It appears that at plausible rates of capital turnover the representative rate of return in the industry would have to be in the range of 22–25 percent, or approximately double the rate of return in manufacturing, to justify on grounds of allocative neutrality the present amount of distinctive tax treatment. A competitive "normal" rate of return of 22–25 percent seems very high, and many economists would doubt its plausibility. Moreover, the evidence presently available, although fragmentary, seems to be consistent with this view. (See Appendix A.) However, a final judgment should await the analysis of a properly designed sample of experience in the industry.

[72] See McDonald, "Percentage Depletion and the Allocation of Resources," pp. 333–35, for an explanation of how these averages were computed from data reported in Internal Revenue Service, *Statistics of Income, Part 2, Corporation Income Tax Returns*, and why these particular years were chosen.

[73] Regarding rates of return, see the discussion in Appendix A. As for rates of capital turnover in the oil and gas industry, an average of .87 was computed for the years 1949–51 and 1953–56, based on corporation income tax returns reporting net income and accompanied by balance sheets and classified in Internal Revenue Service compilations under "Crude Petroleum, Natural Gas and Natural Gasoline" (Mining). As indicated in Appendix A in connection with rates of return derived fom this sample, the data in the above classification are dominated by the results of foreign operations of American companies and hence are not representative of the industry as a whole. However, it was later ascertained that if all returns accompanied by claims for foreign tax credit are eliminated from the sample, the average rate of capital turnover in the remainder of the sample is, at .83, only slightly different from that for the whole classification. (Data adjusted for foreign tax credit claims were supplied by the Statistics Division, Internal Revenue Service.) Although the remainder of the original sample, consisting of about 1,500 small firms accounting for less than 10 percent of total oil and gas production, could hardly be regarded as representative of the industry, the small difference in the average rate of capital turnover suggests that a representative rate for the industry would very likely lie in the range covered by Table 9.

Quite aside from the empirical problem that the foregoing analysis poses, objections may be raised to key parts of the model. The model implicitly assumes that the two industries being compared are the only relevant industries and that they are mutually independent. In other words, neither industry is assumed to buy any inputs from any other industry, so that sales receipts are the same as value added. This level of abstraction seems appropriate to the simple comparison made in both the model developed here and that of Harberger. But it is not appropriate for designing a system of tax rate differentials that would make the corporate income tax generally neutral in its effect on resource allocation. For the latter purpose, capital turnover should be computed on the basis of value added rather than sales receipts. This follows from the fact that if all values added were in consequence of a tax increased by the same percentage, all prices would be increased by the same percentage regardless of the input-output pattern.[74] If the neutrality problem were formulated in general terms and capital turnover ratios computed on the basis of values added by industry, the results indicated in Table 9 might be significantly different.[75]

Other objections may be raised to the model developed here: First, the assumption that rates of return are fully restored by complete adjustment to the corporate income tax implies the underlying assumption that the supply of capital is perfectly elastic with respect to the after-tax return on capital. Most economists would

[74] Considering substitution effects only, a uniform value added tax is widely regarded as a "neutral" tax.

[75] Data supplied in Daniel Creamer and others, *Capital in Manufacturing and Mining* (Princeton University Press, 1960), pp. 57, 81, and 105, are the basis for an estimate that the ratio of value added to total capital *excluding* land in the extractive phase of the oil and gas industry in 1947 (the most recent available year) was .44. The corresponding ratio for manufacturing, *including* land in total capital, was .65. The Creamer data do not provide a basis for adjusting the oil and gas ratio for the inclusion of land in capital, although, as Creamer notes, land is an important part of the total capital used in the industry. If the oil and gas ratio adjusted for land in capital is as low as .35, and if the "normal" rate of return on total capital in manufacturing is taken to be 10 percent (McDonald, "Percentage Depletion and the Allocation of Resources," p. 335), then substitution of these values in the formula for "e" indicates that the present degree of distinctive tax treatment of the oil and gas industry would be supported if the latter industry's "normal" rate of return is approximately 16 percent on total capital. For a fuller discussion of the Creamer data, see McDonald, "Percentage Depletion and Tax Neutrality," pp. 318–19, note 20.

regard this as unrealistic. Strictly speaking, however, that assumption is not made in the model. Constancy of after-tax rates of return follows from other conditions assumed in the model. It is premised on the proposition that risk assumption is a cost; other conditions of the model require that total output be unchanged by the tax in the long run and that the capital-output ratio remain constant. All these conditions cannot be satisfied unless before-tax rates of return rise high enough to leave after-tax rates of return at the same level as before the tax was imposed. The underlying assumption is not that the supply of capital is perfectly elastic—any degree of elasticity may be assumed—but that a given quantity of capital will be supplied only at a given after-tax rate of return. The key proposition is that risk assumption is a cost that remains just as high at the margin after the tax is imposed as before. (This point is developed further below.)

Second, one may object to the assumption of a constant capital-output ratio in each industry. The issue is not whether capital-output ratios are in fact historically constant. Of course, they are not. The question is whether these ratios would change as a result of the tax. There is good reason to believe that they would. With a tax imposed on the return to capital but not on the return to other factors, the altered pattern of net returns would tend to induce a substitution of labor for capital, which would be associated with a decline in capital-output ratios. The inducement to make the substitution would be stronger in those industries in which the return on capital is high relative to the return to all factors of production. But this is merely another way in which a flat-rate corporation income tax may not be neutral. To induce the substitution of labor for capital—and to do it differentially among industries—when there has been no change in relative real marginal productivities is to induce a misallocation of resources. As was explained above, fixed capital-output ratios were assumed in order to focus on a single measure of resource allocation—change in relative prices—rather than two partial measures—change in factor combinations *and* change in relative prices. Without that assumption misallocations would show up in factor markets as well as in product markets.

Third, in abstracting from all taxes except the corporation income tax, the model ignores the fact that in reality there is a noncorporate sector of industry that is not subject to the tax. Resources can escape from the corporate to the noncorporate sector, thus reducing the kinds of absolute and relative price changes allegedly necessary to shift the tax forward. Again, this is merely another possible form of misallocation. If the relative real economies of the corporate form are unaltered, to induce a flow of resources out of the corporate sector, especially in those cases involving a high ratio of return on capital to total factor returns, is to induce a misallocation of resources. If no noncorporate sector is taken account of in the model, misallocation focuses on changes in relative prices.

Fourth, the model ignores the fact that the corporate income tax may be shifted backward. In the case of backward shifting to labor, if mobility of labor in the long run is assumed, the tax would tend to induce a movement of labor out of those industries that are characterized by a high ratio of return on capital to total factor returns and into other industries. With no change in the relative real marginal productivities of labor among industries, the result is a misallocation induced by the tax. Backward shifting to the owners of land is another matter. For some kinds of mineral production, there is no alternative use of land. For others, the use of land to extract minerals does not significantly interfere with other uses. Oil and gas are often produced under one of the latter conditions. In such cases, a corporation income tax can be shifted backward to landowners without changing the most efficient combination of resources. If economic rents are more significant in the total costs of the oil and gas industry than in other industries, this constitutes a major qualification of the argument that a flat-rate corporation income tax may tend to discriminate, in resource allocation terms, against the oil and gas industry.

THE MUSGRAVE THESIS. One of the strongest objections to the model developed here centers on the proposition that risk assumption is a cost that remains unaffected by the terms of the tax. Richard A. Musgrave[76] has argued that with perfect loss offsets—including, if the taxpayer has no net income against which to charge a loss, a

---

[76] Richard A. Musgrave, *The Theory of Public Finance* (McGraw-Hill, 1959), Chap. 14. The chapter draws heavily on an earlier article, Evsey D. Domar and Richard A. Musgrave, "Proportional Income Taxation and Risk-Taking," *Quarterly Journal of Economics*, Vol. 58 (May 1944), pp. 387–422. See also Musgrave, "Another Look at Depletion," p. 206.

direct subsidy equal to a loss multiplied by the effective tax rate—a flat-rate tax on the return to capital reduces risk and returns proportionately, so that the return per unit of resources risked remains the same as in the absence of the tax. In effect, the Treasury becomes a silent partner in the investment process, sharing proportionately in gains and losses from the process. Suppose, for example, that the tax rate is 50 percent. The private investor may keep only one-half of any positive earnings he may realize, but he risks losing only one-half of whatever outlays he may make on capital account. The rate of return on investment, which appears to be lower because of the tax, is in effect the same rate of return as before the tax was imposed on the private investor's outlay at risk.[77] Accordingly, the tax may cut the apparent rate of return in half without reducing the investor's outlays. There is no need for the before-tax rate of return to rise in order to maintain the flow of capital.

Musgrave goes further and argues that imposition of a flat-rate income tax with perfect loss offsets would, under the assumption of diminishing marginal utility of income as income increases, increase risk-taking. In other words, the average degree of riskiness of investments would be increased, or the acceptable return on an investment of any given degree of riskiness would be decreased. This follows from the assumption about the marginal utility of income and the fact that the tax would reduce the income of investors. With a lower income and a higher marginal utility of income, an investor would be willing to assume more risk to get a given amount of income. Thus the tax might lead to a relative, as well as an absolute, reduction in the acceptable return on relatively risky investments.

Musgrave notes a number of significant qualifications to his

[77] Where loss offsets take the form of the privilege of expensing capital outlays as they are made against whatever taxable income may be available (e.g., the expensing of unsuccessful exploration costs in the oil and gas industry), the effect is to reduce the average amount of capital used per unit of output. If this effect is fully reflected in the capital turnover ratio used in the model developed here, no further adjustment for risk reduction need be made, since the required rate of return on the capital actually at risk is unchanged according to Musgrave's argument. Where loss offsets take the form of tax refunds, when and as literal accounting losses occur under orthodox methods of depreciation, the offsets themselves are subject to discount at the time an investment is made, since the timing and circumstances of tax refunds are subject to some uncertainty. The prospect of loss offsets at an effective tax rate of 50 percent is thus not quite the same as making a net investment equal to one-half the gross outlay.

thesis:[78] First, the analysis applies to investment situations representing pure Knightian risk, that is, situations in which there are known probability distributions of possible returns on investment. Situations involving uncertainty are not analyzed, although Musgrave notes that such situations might lead to different results than those involving pure risk.

Second, a related qualification stems from the treatment of each investment decision as if it were discrete—as if the results of a given decision were of no consequence for the ability of the investor to make subsequent decisions on the same basis. In fact, of course, business investment decisions involve the continuity of the decision-making unit.[79] Even partially offset losses jeopardize the business unit's freedom of choice among alternatives, its credit-worthiness and possibly its survival. It is extremely doubtful, therefore, that an income tax with perfect loss offsets can be viewed as affecting symmetrically the gain and loss components of a prospective net income distribution.

Third, Musgrave defines the return on investment to exclude, in effect, any sort of reward other than that for taking chances on a known probability distribution. "Loss" is defined as anything less than zero income. If the return on investment is assumed to compensate for investment effort (entrepreneurship) or any other real sacrifice that does not give rise to a tax reduction, then loss should be defined as anything less than some positive return on investment reflecting the real social costs of capital formation.

Fourth, Musgrave recognizes that the income effect, which allegedly would lead an individual investor to assume more risk for a given prospective income, would not necessarily apply to corporation managers. The possibility that for both personal and corporate investors a reduction of income would increase the marginal disutility of risk-taking is ignored.

Finally, with reference to empirical applications of the loss-offset hypothesis, it must be noted that loss offsets under past and present income tax arrangements in the United States are less than perfect,

---

[78] Musgrave, *The Theory of Public Finance*, pp. 328–33, especially, although other qualifications are noted in the text.

[79] This and the remaining observations concerning the present qualification are those of the author and not of Musgrave. They are, however, suggested by Musgrave's discussion of qualifications.

even when "loss" is defined in the strict accounting sense of less-than-zero income. The availability of loss offsets to the investor depends on the form they take (see note 77) and on past, present, and possible future circumstances. Their applicability to any investment project is itself subject to uncertainty, a fact which compounds the uncertainties associated with purchasing real assets. The present rules governing loss offsets in this country probably discriminate against and thus discourage new entrants into risky industries. They thus increase the realized rate of return necessary to attract capital at the margin relative to what would be necessary with perfect loss offsets.

In view of these qualifications of the loss-offset argument, and in the absence of empirical evidence to support it, it is difficult to believe that the introduction of the corporation income tax and associated loss-offset provisions in the United States significantly reduced the acceptable rate of return on risky investments. On the other hand, it seems undeniable that acceptable rates of return would be lower with loss offsets than without them. Further improvement of loss-offset provisions should therefore reduce any lack of neutrality stemming from differential riskiness; and, on grounds of feasibility at least, such an approach to reducing this lack is superior to a general system of tax differentials.

There are two criticisms of the argument presented here that may be directed against the comparison of the oil and gas industry with manufacturing as a whole. First, the procedure ignores the wide range of rates of return and rates of capital turnover to be found *within* the broad manufacturing category or the total range of economic activities. There may be many types of manufacturing or other industries that on grounds of riskiness and/or capital intensity would be equal or better candidates for distinctive tax treatment than the oil and gas industry. There is no presumption otherwise in the author's thesis. The particular comparison was made because the distinctive tax provisions applying to the oil and gas industry have been attacked on the grounds that they are peculiarly deneutralizing, and manufacturing industries as a class have been used as the standard of comparison in making that attack. The author has argued, at the same level of abstraction, that the distinctive tax provisions may not be deneutralizing.

Second, it may be pointed out that the tax system as a whole is quite unneutral and that it would be impossible to prove that adjusting only one part of it as it applies to one class of industry would improve the general allocative efficiency of the economy. This is a valid argument. But it is double-edged; it may be used equally well to challenge the thesis that distinctive tax provisions in the oil and gas industry are peculiarly deneutralizing and damaging to general allocative efficiency. The criticism serves most constructively to emphasize the proposition that if it is general allocative neutrality we want in our tax system, the system must be appraised as a whole.[80]

To summarize, there is reason to believe that the oil and gas industry, in its finding-production phase, is a relatively risky industry, but the evidence is subject to conflicting interpretations. Harberger and others, using a model that takes no explicit account of capital turnover, have argued that no plausible degree of relative riskiness could eliminate the apparent lack of neutrality of the differential tax treatment of income from oil and gas production. (For discussion of this point, see the Summary of the Conference of Experts below, p. 122.) But the analysis used here, based on a model that explicitly incorporates capital turnover as a determinant, suggests that relative riskiness in an industry would require some differential tax treatment to be consistent with allocative neutrality. However, there are many objections to this analytical model, and in the nature of the case it is impossible to prove that the oil and gas industry is risky enough to justify the present amount of differential treatment. We can only say that if the industry is especially risky, and if a flat-rate income tax tends to be shifted in the long run in the sense that rates of return are restored to pre-tax levels, it may be possible to defend a differentially low effective rate of taxation in the industry on the grounds of allocative neutrality as between the industry and manufacturing as a whole—especially if oil and gas production is also relatively capital intensive. Unfortunately, the unsatisfactory state of both factual information and the theory of incidence militates against a definite conclusion here.

[80] See note 61 above regarding Harberger's explicit recognition of this fact.

CHAPTER IV

Oil and Gas as Wasting Assets

OIL AND GAS MAY BE REGARDED as "wasting assets" in two senses: (1) They belong to that class of natural resources called "fund resources," the absolute quantity of which in the crust of the earth diminishes unit for unit with extraction and use, there being no operating natural or human mechanism for replacing the units consumed. Discussion of this matter is reserved for the immediately following section, devoted to oil and gas conservation in relation to distinctive tax provisions. (2) Oil and gas deposits being exploited are to their owners wasting assets in the same sense that any item of real capital may be a wasting asset to its owner; that is, use in production ordinarily diminishes its real capital value. It is in the latter sense that wasting assets are considered here.

Investment and Net Income

It may be helpful to begin with a brief statement of the theory of capital in relation to the determination of net income. A real capital asset—a nonhuman, man-made, or man-appropriated instrument of production—has two aspects: the "thing" and the economic value. The nature and quantity of the "thing" have economic significance only insofar as they are reflected in the economic value. The economic value of the "thing" may be viewed and measured in two

different ways, each having its own peculiar significance: (1) There
is the economic value in the sense of cost price; i.e., the value of that
which must be given up to produce or acquire the "thing." (2)
There is the economic value that is derived by discounting the expected net proceeds[81] from use of the "thing" in production. In a
competitive economy, with discount rates appropriately reflecting
uncertainty, the two measures of value tend to equal each other at
the margin at the time of the act of investment. After the act of investment, however, the two values may diverge, the first then reflecting a sunk cost and the second reflecting different expectations
of net proceeds than were held at the time of investment, in the light
of newly revealed but initially unforeseen events.

For the moment leaving aside the question of divergent cost and
value-in-use of a capital asset, there is the question of what happens
to the initial value in consequence of use. In the case of most capital
instruments, use of the "thing" in production (or even mere passage
of time) gradually diminishes its income-producing powers and
hence its value. Such a reduction in value may result from wearing
out, from obsolescence, or from reduction in the stock of the "thing."
Thus, most machines wear out or become obsolescent; appropriated
deposits of oil and gas (and other items of inventory capital) diminish in physical quantity with production. In either case, the
process of production ordinarily involves the destruction of some
capital value. Accordingly, the measure of net production (and of
net economic income) is value added—the difference between gross
value created and value destroyed in the process of creation.

The income-generating process may be viewed as an investment
cycle. To begin the cycle, an investor exchanges generalized command over wealth and current output for an asset of a particular
kind. The exchange being a voluntary one, the value given up
approximates the *presumed* value-in-use of the "thing" at the time of
acquisition. Production now begins, and net proceeds (as defined
above) are realized from use of the capital instrument. If over the
full life of the asset the investor's expectations are exactly fulfilled,
the initial judgment as to the value-in-use of the asset is validated.
This is to say that the total net proceeds exceed the initial cost of the
asset by such an amount, distributed in such a way in time, as to

---

[81] Gross proceeds net of all costs except allowance for capital consumption. In
current business parlance, the term for net proceeds is "net cash flow."

yield the investor his expected rate of return. The excess of net proceeds over initial cost is the absolute net income of the investor, for it measures the increase in the investor's command over wealth and current output from beginning to end of the investment cycle. Accordingly the *periodic* net income during the investment cycle can be measured by making deductions from each period's net proceeds representing that period's share of the initial cost of the asset. The sum of the periodic deductions equals the initial cost.

But what if the investor's expectations are not exactly realized, the flow of net proceeds being larger or smaller than expected at the time of investment? In such a case, the "true" initial value of the capital asset (seen in retrospect) will have been greater or less than the outlay made to acquire it.

Does this change in any way the appropriate manner of measuring the investor's net income? Obviously it does not. His net income is still the increase in his command over wealth and current output from beginning to end of the investment cycle. If expectations are not realized exactly, it means, of course, that net income is larger or smaller than expected. Divergence of cost and value-in-use of the capital asset is a *reflection* of divergence of net income from the expected. Value-in-use therefore cannot be used to measure the net income. If value-in-use *per se* were the basis for capital consumption deductions, measured net income would always equal expected net income (because allowed for in the discounting process)—an obvious absurdity. Value-in-use of a capital asset *per se* has no place in the measurement of net income from investment; it is significant only as a measure of the worth of an expected stream of net proceeds to a prospective buyer or seller of rights to such proceeds. Initial cost *per se* is the economically valid basis for measuring capital consumption in production, hence net income from production.

The oil and gas industry (and to a lesser degree perhaps the other mineral industries) differs from, say, manufacturing in that in exploration-development drilling there need be no close relation between particular investment outlays and the initial value-in-use of the asset acquired for the outlay. Indeed, it is this lack of relation which underlies the uncertainty peculiar to the industry. It cannot be said, therefore, that for individual investments in the search for oil the initial outlay is the same as the initial value-in-use acquired.

Aside from the implications of riskiness already discussed, does this fact in any way affect the economic validity of initial cost as the appropriate basis for measuring capital consumption and hence net income from production? The answer must, in general, again be no. There are, however, some qualifying considerations.

Consider first the negative side. However uncertain may be the outcome of particular investments in the search for oil and gas, the fact remains that the net income of investors, individually and collectively, is the difference between their command over wealth and current output at the beginning and at the end of the investment cycle. That difference is measured by net proceeds from investment less initial outlay. The peculiar risks in investment mean only that particular investments may yield net incomes of unusually widely varying amounts: from the amount of the investment outlay with negative sign to almost any positive amount. If oil and gas explorers used the capitalized value of discoveries as the basis of deductions for capital consumption, all actual discoveries resulting in production would yield precisely the net income implicit in the discount factor used—the absurd result previously alluded to. Even more absurd, perhaps, those making no discoveries would register no losses.

Measures of Capital Consumption

In actual practice, firms and individuals engaged in finding and producing oil and gas measure income for internal accounting purposes in the economically valid manner by deducting from net proceeds amounts for capital consumption based on initial outlays. But the issue here is the appropriate basis of a capital consumption deduction for income tax purposes. With regard to the oil and gas industry, it is possible to make a case for capital consumption deductions for tax purposes based on "discovery value," i.e., the capitalized expected net proceeds at the time of discovery.

The case is based on two propositions: First, it must be presumed that over any reasonable period of time (say, five years) the total outlays by the industry in search of oil and gas are matched by total value of discoveries,[82] expected proceeds from the latter being ap-

[82] Net of the royalty interest, of course.

propriately discounted to reflect uncertainty. On the assumption of investor rationality and free exit and entry, if the value of discoveries should be greater than (or less than) outlays for any extended period, funds would be attracted (or repelled). The tendency, therefore, would continually be toward equality of aggregate outlays and aggregate value of discoveries. Therefore, discovery value would tend to be the same as outlays for exploration for all productive properties in the aggregate. Second, due to uncertainty of success in drilling, some investors in the search for oil and gas may lack sufficient past, current, or subsequent income to derive the full tax benefit from deductions for unsuccessful exploration effort. If so, and if firms and individuals in the industry are limited to the amount of actual outlays in taking deductions for capital consumption, the total deductions taken for tax purposes would be less than the costs incurred.

Under these conditions, which might obtain with the present system of less than perfect loss offsets, the income tax would fall more heavily on net income from the oil and gas industry than on that from less risky industries. On the other hand, if discovery value were the basis allowed for capital consumption deductions, total deductions in the long run would correspond to total outlays; and those taking the deductions presumably would have enough income to derive full tax benefit from them. Hence the income tax would not discriminate against the riskier industry. One may object to the inequity of allowing one taxpayer to get the benefits of a capital consumption deduction representing outlays made by another, less fortunate, taxpayer. A more equitable arrangement would be for the Treasury to equalize the position of the taxpayer with insufficient income to give him the full benefits of loss offsets by directly contributing to him an amount equal to the effective tax rate times the uncovered loss. Here we are concerned solely with the purely economic question of possible discrimination against the relatively risky industry considered as a whole.[83]

Of course, to justify discovery value capital consumption allowances on this basis, one must accept the proposition that discovery

---

[83] It may be noted, incidentally, that in comparison with a system of perfect loss offsets discovery value depletion would widen the range of possible net incomes after taxes from investments in the search for oil and gas and probably would discourage entry.

values of oil and gas deposits do in fact tend to equal actual outlays in the long run; and one must logically assume that any and all capital consumption deductions based on actual discovery outlays in the industry would be disallowed.[84] If deductions based on actual discovery outlays were not disallowed in connection with discovery value depletion, total deductions would exceed total outlays, and net income would be understated for tax purposes by the amount of the excess. There may be other grounds on which to defend capital consumption allowances based on discovery value *plus* discovery outlays, but the argument that such allowances correctly measure actual capital consumption is logically unacceptable.

Increasing Costs and Capital Consumption Allowances

It is sometimes argued that the oil and gas industry faces increasing costs in the ever more intensive and extensive search for new reserves.[85] This argument, often made to defend distinctive tax provisions,[86] raises the issue of replacement cost as the appropriate basis for capital consumption allowances. Use of replacement cost has been defended as a means of eliminating the distorting effects of changes in the general price level.[87] But to defend it on grounds of increasing real costs in a particular industry is a different matter.

There are two valid economic bases for rejecting such an argument for capital consumption allowances based on replacement cost. In the first place, as shown earlier, the net income from each

[84] For purchasers of proven properties, presumably acquisition costs would equal values acquired in each individual case, except when mistakes were made. Hence the distinction between outlay and value of acquisition would be of no practical significance to them.

[85] See, for example, Mid-Continent Oil and Gas Association, *op. cit.*, p. 16. The question of increasing costs in the oil industry is discussed in Appendix D.

[86] Mid-Continent Oil and Gas Association, *op. cit.*, p. 15, for example.

[87] Use of initial costs as the basis of capital consumption allowances in the presence of inflation not only leads to overstatement of real income for tax purposes by business in general; it results in tax discrimination against the industries using relatively long-lived equipment. Militating against attempts to adjust capital consumption allowances for inflation are the well-known problems of administrative complexity and the construction of price indexes free of distortion from changes in quality of the underlying goods. One may add, incidentally, in favor of the conventional procedures that the effects of inflation on the real tax burden of business are an aid to stabilizing fiscal policy: inflation produces an automatic increase in real tax rates.

investment cycle is correctly measured on the basis of the initial outlays in the cycle. To use replacement cost in the face of increasing real costs is to burden the net proceeds of one cycle with costs that in principle have nothing to do with earning those net proceeds and that in practice result in an understatement of that cycle's net income. Each cycle stems from an investment decision in which necessary capital outlays and expected net proceeds are compared. The relevant outlays are those which presumably will result in the net proceeds in question. Possible higher outlays in future are totally irrelevant to the decision, and precisely because they are irrelevant to the expected net income that shapes the decision. At the end of a cycle, the investor is free to replace his worn-out asset or to invest in some other type of asset as he chooses. He is not permanently committed to any particular kind of asset or industry. He can consider each successive round of investment and recovery on its own merits—that is, in the light of its own costs and expected net proceeds. So real replacement cost—higher, lower, or the same—has nothing to do with determining the true economic net income from a particular investment.

In the second place, the interests of allocative efficiency require that increasing real costs in a particular industry be fully reflected in the prices of that industry's product. If replacement cost is used as the basis of tax allowances for capital consumption, the result in the case of an industry with increasing costs is an artificially reduced income tax liability in each investment cycle. The consequence, other things being equal, is lower relative prices than otherwise would obtain in the industry and a greater use of productive resources than ought to obtain on the basis of real costs and returns; for at the margin, real costs (including the industry's "appropriate" share of the real burden of government) exceed the real product of resources used.

Conclusion

The foregoing discussion leads to these conclusions: (1) in the light of capital and income theory, initial cost must be adjudged the economically appropriate basis for capital consumption allowances. Economically speaking, it is not the capital instrument itself that is consumed in the process of production; it is the value of the resources exchanged for the instrument at the outset of the investment cycle. (2) In certain circumstances, such as those in an industry characterized by uncertainty in the investment process, initial capitalized value of a capital instrument may logically be used as a measure of capital consumption, but only as a *substitute* for initial outlay and not as a *supplement* to the latter. The circumstances that may justify use of initial capitalized value in lieu of initial outlay appear to be characteristic of the oil and gas industry. (3) The use of replacement cost as the basis of tax allowances for capital consumption on the grounds of increasing real costs in an industry is logically unsound and economically undesirable.

If these conclusions are correct, the distinctive tax provisions applying to income from oil and gas production do not provide an accurate measure of capital consumption in the industry. Percentage depletion was originally introduced as an administratively feasible substitute for discovery value (initial capitalized value) depletion; and the typical percentage depletion deduction may still be reasonably representative of discovery value.[88] But use of percentage depletion does not preclude the additional deduction from taxable income of nearly all capital outlays actually made in the search for, and development of, oil and gas deposits. To the extent that percentage depletion approximates discovery value, the cost-based deductions are excess deductions on grounds of income theory. Moreover, the expensing of dry hole costs and intangible costs of drilling productive wells has the effect of charging the greater part of replacement costs against current income.

All this was said before in different form: in the oil and gas industry, typical total deductions for tax purposes exceed total costs actually incurred, and some of the principal deductions may be treated as ordinary operating expenses. It is the conclusion of the present section that these practices do not represent an economically sound way to measure capital consumption in the industry.

---

[88] On crude oil, with a recent average price in the United States of about $3.00 a barrel and a maximum percentage depletion rate of 27.5, the maximum depletion deduction is about $0.83 a barrel. Recent prices for crude oil reserves in various stages of development are reported to be in the range of $0.90 to $1.25 a barrel. (Mid-Continent Oil and Gas Association, *op. cit.*, p. 20.)

CHAPTER V

Conservation of Oil and Gas

"CONSERVATION"[89] has several different meanings. In some contexts, e.g., referring to a "scenic wonder" or historical site, conservation implies nonconsumption or preservation intact of the resource in question. Obviously, such a definition has no significance in the analysis of problems which presume the consumption of resources. Ciriacy-Wantrup[90] uses the term to mean a reduction in current use of a resource with a view to increasing future use—a deliberate act of postponement of consumption. To him, the "state" of conservation is the degree to which current use is restrained in the interest of future use. The "optimum state" of conservation is that which maxi-

---

[89] The literature on the subject of oil and gas conservation and regulatory institutions is quite extensive. Some of the more important works are: Erich W. Zimmermann, *Conservation in the Production of Petroleum* (Yale University Press, 1957); Anthony Scott, *Natural Resources: The Economics of Conservation* (University of Toronto Press, 1955); S. V. Ciriacy-Wantrup, *Resource Conservation: Economics and Policies* (University of California Press, 1952); M. G. de Chazeau and A. E. Kahn, *Integration and Competition in the Petroleum Industry* (Yale University Press, 1959); S. E. Buckley (ed.), *Petroleum Conservation* (American Institute of Mining and Metallurgical Engineers, 1951); E. V. Rostow, *A National Policy for the Oil and Gas Industry* (Yale University Press, 1948); Wallace F. Lovejoy and I. James Pikl, Jr. (eds.), *Essays on Petroleum Conservation Regulation* (Southern Methodist University, 1960). Much of the following section is based on James W. McKie and Stephen L. McDonald, "Petroleum Conservation in Theory and Practice," *Quarterly Journal of Economics*, Vol. 76 (February 1962), pp. 98–121.

[90] *Op. cit.* See also his "Private Enterprise and Conservation," *Journal of Farm Economics*, Vol. 24 (February 1942), especially p. 79.

mizes the present value of the expected net proceeds (discounted at an appropriate rate) from use of the resource in question. In the conservation statutes of most of the oil and gas producing states, "conservation" means the avoidance of waste of the resource in question. Waste is usually defined in these statutes in terms of physical escape or loss of units of the resource, without reference to the cost in terms of other resources (particularly labor and capital) of avoiding such escape or loss.[91] In this study the term "conservation" is used to mean an optimum time-rate of use of a particular resource; or, put in negative terms, the avoidance of waste, including waste of labor and capital, associated with a faulty time-rate of use of a particular resource. Under this definition, conservation means continually maximizing the present value of the expected net proceeds from use of the resource in question, expected net proceeds being discounted at a competitively determined market rate of interest. The definition thus coincides with Ciriacy-Wantrup's concept of an "optimum state" of conservation. Moreover, the definition of conservation used here implies, as is intended, that the theory of conservation is but an application of the theory of capital.[92]

"Stock" and "Flow" Resources

For certain limited analytical purposes, it is useful to make a conceptual distinction between "stock" and "flow" resources. In the

[91] The Texas statute, for instance, defines conservation of oil and gas in terms of avoidance of waste and specifies that "waste" includes: "the operation of any oil well or wells with an inefficient gas-oil ratio. . . ," "underground waste or loss however caused. . . ," "permitting any natural gas well to burn wastefully," "the creation of unnecessary fire hazards," "escape into the open air . . . of natural gas in excess of the amount which is necessary in the efficient drilling or operation of [a] well," and "the production of crude petroleum oil in excess of transportation or market facilities or reasonable market demand." (*Revised Civil Statutes of Texas*, Title 102, Article 6014, cited by Wallace F. Lovejoy, "Conservation Regulation: The Economic and Legal Setting," in Lovejoy and Pikl, *op. cit.*, pp. 29–30). It may be noted that the use of such qualifying terms as "wastefully," "unnecessary," "inefficient," and "reasonable" actually leaves to administrative officials the problem of deciding what weight to give to cost in terms of other resources in the effort to avoid waste of oil and gas.

[92] This is the central argument of Scott, *op. cit.* For an excellent short statement of modern conservation theory in the light of Scott's and Ciriacy-Wantrup's contributions, see I. James Pikl, "Conservation: Its Economic Meaning and Significance," in Lovejoy and Pikl, *op. cit.*, pp. 8–23.

case of the former, purely conceived, there is postulated some original stock or fund of the resource in nature, a fund which *cannot be* increased or reproduced in any part by man and *is not* increased or reproduced in any part by nature, and which, therefore, decreases *pari passu* with consumption. In contrast, a pure flow resource is one that is renewable at some level of use, either by natural occurrence or in consequence of deliberate human action in cooperation with nature. But this distinction is not an adequate basis for a theory of conservation separate from the general theory of capital. With a pure stock resource, assuming the stock is appropriated and its dimensions fully known, the conservation problem is simply one of distributing consumption of the stock over time. The solution calls for anticipating prices and costs over time and selecting a suitable rate of discount. With a pure flow resource, the conservation problem is simply how much of other resources to invest, from time to time, in renewal, assuming that human action has a bearing on the rate of renewal.[93] In other words, conservation of a flow resource is a simple investment problem requiring, as in all such cases, anticipating prices and costs over time and selecting a suitable rate of discount. In essence, the conservation of both stock and flow resources requires a present sacrifice of possible consumption in the interest of future consumption. The sacrifice is economically desirable if its value is equal to, or less than, the discounted present worth of the expected increase in future consumption. The connection of conservation theory with the general theory of capital thus becomes clear.

In reality, no natural resource has, or has ever had, the characteristics of a pure stock resource as defined above. Those usually called stock resources, such as mineral resources, actually combine the characteristics of stock and flow resources. The total physical quantity of minerals like oil and gas "originally" deposited in the crust of the earth is, so far as is known, fixed forever; there is no known mechanism presently at work to reproduce any part of that original stock. But the *known and appropriated* stock of oil and gas is some small fraction of that original total—how small a fraction being unknowable because the original physical stock itself is un-

---

[93] Needless to say, if human action has no bearing on the rate of renewal of a flow resource, there is no specifiable conservation problem.

known. At any given time, the unknown and unappropriated portion of the original physical stock is subject to discovery and appropriation by human endeavor. The process of discovery and appropriation is analogous to renewal of a flow resource. (In fact, of course, the known stock of oil and gas has been more or less continually renewed and enlarged throughout the life thus far of the industry.) Consequently, conservation of oil and gas involves two interdependent decisions: the rate of use of the existing known stock and the amount of investment in renewal of the known stock. The investment criteria are the same in each case, although the decisions must be made simultaneously and as one, since each decision affects the data on which the other is based. The two decisions, properly made, lead to the equation of cost and product on two different margins: that of intensive exploitation of existing supplies and that of extensive investment in sources of new supply.

No special problem of expectations is introduced by the possibility of sudden exhaustion of the remaining unknown and unappropriated original deposits. Oil and gas, like other minerals, exist in varying grades and varying degrees of accessibility and recoverability. Long before physical exhaustion could occur, increasing costs at the extensive margin would drive up prices, push out the intensive margin of exploitation, encourage technical innovations in the discovery and recovery processes, discourage current consumption out of existing stocks, and place a growing premium on the development of substitute materials. Such economic reactions would at once lengthen the life of existing appropriated stocks and provide a mechanism for the orderly reduction of the role of oil and gas in the total resource-use pattern. It is the role of conservation as defined here to cause the costs of renewal at the margin to be reflected in relative prices so that oil and gas (and other such resources) may last as economic resources as long as they can pay their own way, and no longer. It follows then that the pricing mechanism is critical to the conservation of oil and gas. Either under- or over-pricing of oil and gas currently would lead to something other than the optimum time-rate of use of these minerals and hence would violate the principles of conservation.

State Conservation Regulations

Although the discussion above suggests the possible conservation effects of distinctive tax provisions applying to the oil and gas industry, conclusions should be withheld until after a discussion of state conservation regulations.[94] These regulations produce some economic effects that modify the consequences of distinctive tax provisions.

The history of various state efforts to prevent waste in the exploitation of oil and gas deposits extends back into the late nineteenth century; but the complex regulations that operate today in the principal producing states[95] originated in the chaotic conditions of the early 1930's, when the unrestricted development of several huge discoveries, chiefly the great East Texas Field, in the midst of general economic depression entailed vast losses of oil and gas and severely depressed prices. Under the "rule of capture," still the basic legal doctrine pertaining to ownership of fugacious resources, it is in the interests of separate owners of surface rights over a given newly discovered oil and/or gas deposit to drill as many wells as possible as soon as possible, and to produce from those wells at the maximum feasible rate, in order to make sure of protecting (or, rather, maximizing) their property interests.[96]

[94] For an excellent short survey of state conservation laws and practices in the United States, see Lovejoy, *op. cit.*, pp. 24–47. The following discussion draws heavily on this source.

[95] The regulations naturally differ from state to state, but they are essentially similar in purpose and approach in Texas, Louisiana, Oklahoma, and New Mexico, which together produce about two-thirds of the nation's output of crude oil. All of these states have laws providing for restriction of production to "market demand." California, the third largest producer in the nation, with about one-tenth of the total, is noteworthy for its lack of a comprehensive conservation law. Texas, the principal producing state, accounting for about 35 percent of total national output of crude oil, has an elaborate system of conservation regulation, but it is like California in having no provision for pooling of acreage for purposes of forming minimum-size drilling units. Partly for this reason, and partly because of Texas' dominant role in national production of crude oil, the Texas approach to conservation regulation is often singled out for critical discussion.

[96] Obviously, in cases where one operator owns all the surface rights, there is no motivation to over-drill and wastefully exploit a deposit. It is this consideration, of course, which underlies the desirability, in principle, of compulsory unitization of oil and gas reservoirs for purposes of development and production. For an analysis of the problems and benefits of compulsory unitization, see Buckley, *op. cit.*, pp. 281–96 and Zimmermann, *op. cit.*, pp. 343–49.

The inevitable results of such an approach to exploitation are: (1) an unnecessarily large investment in drilling and well equipment; (2) premature exhaustion of gas cap drive, if such is present, the gas itself often being allowed to escape or to burn for want of an immediately available means of distribution and sale; (3) uneven drainage in the reservoir, with water and/or gas bypassing and isolating pockets of petroleum, which then become economically unrecoverable; and (4) in cases where production from the field is large enough, depression of prices below full costs of development and production. To prevent or minimize such consequences, the principal producing states, except California (see note 95), have instituted regulations designed to prohibit certain kinds of presumably wasteful activities (e.g., flaring of gas and operation of an oil well at an "inefficient" gas-oil ratio), to control the minimum spacing of wells, to limit production to "reasonable market demand," and to allocate allowable production among fields and among wells within fields.[97]

BENEFITS OF STATE REGULATION. The undoubted results of such regulations, most of which have been in operation in the principal producing states for over twenty years, have included genuine reduction of waste, both of recoverable oil and gas and of labor and capital in the development of deposits, greater protection of correlative rights of surface owners, and stabilization of prices.

All of these results, even stabilization of prices, may have been, and probably have been, consistent with conservation as defined for the purposes of this study. Stabilization of prices may have been in the interests of conservation for two reasons: First, it probably has reduced capital rationing to the industry and thus has reduced the financial bias in favor of current as against future production. Owners may easily borrow on the basis of proved reserves in order to finance current operations; investors who feel that future oil and gas prices will be substantially higher than current prices can easily borrow to finance purchases of proven reserves. Thus "waiting" is financially more feasible in consequence of price stabilization. Second, short-run stabilization of prices may make it less difficult to

[97] This list does not exhaust the types of regulations in use. Other significant ones pertain to ratable take from wells within a reservoir by purchasers and unitization for purposes of drilling and production. See Lovejoy, *op. cit.*, p. 31, for a list of types of regulations used by different states.

appraise long-run trends in prices and costs, hence less difficult to make intelligent decisions regarding present vs. future production of oil and gas.

CRITICISMS OF STATE REGULATION. Despite the undoubted and possible conservation benefits of state regulations, the latter have been severely criticized.[98] Not only do criticisms raise questions about the genuine conservation effects of the regulations; they have implications for the possible conservation effects of distinctive tax provisions in the presence of such regulations.

1. It should be noted, first of all, that such superficially wasteful activities as flaring of gas or failure to recover all technically recoverable oil in a reservoir are not necessarily economically wasteful. Blanket prohibition of such activities may impose greater costs in terms of labor and capital than benefits in terms of the value of the oil and gas "saved." If so, the result is not conservation in an economic sense. By imposing unnecessary costs on both present and future production, prohibitions of this sort only hasten the time when it will become uneconomical to extend further the extensive and intensive margins of oil and gas exploration and exploitation. The oil and gas "saved" may thus ultimately be worthless material in the crust of the earth—unsearched-for because unwanted, unwanted because uneconomical, uneconomical because artificially priced out of its markets.

2. It is almost universally agreed, even within the industry, that spacing regulations permit undue density of wells. Operators are moved to drill wells as densely as the regulations allow largely because authorities in the states having "market demand" production control allocate field production allowables partly on the basis of number of wells. Particularly in Texas, it is possible to increase the total allowable production of a field or a lease by increasing the number of wells in production. Thus under that state's basic allocation formula, the so-called "1947 Yardstick,"[99] a 10,000-foot well on

---

[98] The more important works severely criticizing prevailing state conservation practices in part or in whole include: M. W. Watkins, *Oil: Stabilization or Conservation?* (Harper, 1937); E. V. Rostow, *op. cit.;* de Chazeau and Kahn, *op. cit.;* Zimmermann, *op. cit.;* and R. E. Hardwicke, "Oil-Well Spacing Regulations and Protection of Property Rights in Texas," *Texas Law Review,* Vol. 31 (December 1952). Zimmermann and Hardwicke are critical chiefly of spacing regulations.

[99] See McKie and McDonald, *op. cit.,* p. 112.

80 acres has a basic daily allowable of 270 barrels; four 10,000-foot wells on 80 acres (20-acre spacing) have a basic daily allowable totaling 840 barrels. The situation in Texas is made worse by an old court ruling to the effect that, general well-spacing regulations notwithstanding, a leaseholder is entitled to at least one well on his property, no matter how small it may be, and to a production allowable for that well large enough for him to make a profit operating it.[100] From 1940 to 1962 the basic minimum spacing in Texas was 20 acres, although there was a tendency on the part of the regulatory commission (the Texas Railroad Commission) to impose wider spacing in new fields. Yet as late as 1958, some 76 percent of the wells drilled in Texas were on 20-acre spacing or less.[101] In recent years, Louisiana (1960), Oklahoma (1961), and Texas (1962) significantly improved their well-spacing rules by making 40 acres the basic minimum.[102] It is probably still true, however, that in general too many wells are drilled in the United States to produce efficiently the nation's output of oil and gas. The result is to burden both present and future production with unnecessary costs and to hinder, to that extent, the optimum time-rate of use of both known and yet-to-be-discovered deposits of oil and gas.

3. Restriction of production to "reasonable market demand" in the major producing states (except California) also probably has the effect of burdening the industry with unnecessary costs quite aside from the matter of well spacing. This stems from the practice, again principally in Texas, of exempting discovery wells for a maximum of 18 months, wells in secondary recovery projects, and so-called marginal wells (legislatively defined in terms of production capabilities[103]) from production restrictions under the "market de-

[100] Zimmermann, op. cit., p. 340, citing Railroad Commission v. Humble Oil and Refining Co., 193 S. W. 2d 824.832 (1946). However, it appears that in two recent cases—the Normanna Field case (Railroad Commission v. Atlantic Refining Co., 346 S. W. 2d 801, 1961) and the Port Acres Field case (Halbouty v. Railroad Commission, 357 S.W. 2d 801, 1962), the Supreme Court of Texas has struck down the earlier rule when it allows the small-tract well operator to recover more than his "fair share" of oil and gas deposits being tapped.

[101] McKie and McDonald, op. cit., p. 114, citing Oil and Gas Journal (Jan. 18, 1960), p. 43.

[102] The Louisiana and Oklahoma basic minima are associated with production allowable formulas, in which spacing is a major factor. For an explanation of these formulas, see McKie and McDonald, op. cit., pp. 116–18.

[103] A "marginal well" in Texas is statutorily defined as one capable of producing no more than 10 barrels a day from a depth of 2,000 feet or less, or larger amounts at

mand" rule. About half of Texas' wells are exempt, chiefly because of "marginal" status. The other half of the wells, capable of relatively low-cost flowing production, must bear the full burden of production restriction. Since 1958 they have been held to a third or less of their basic allowable, so that, despite their relatively high production capabilities, they have been permitted to produce less than 60 percent of the state's total output of crude oil.[104] Restriction of production to "market demand," estimated on the implicit assumption of the current price, obviously lends support to the current price. Placing the burden of restriction on the lower-cost producers in effect forces inefficiencies upon them and raises their costs relative to the costs of the marginal producers. Prices are protected from undermining by relatively low-cost oil, but rates of return from discovery and development of new flowing deposits are restricted. The general result is that crude oil prices are kept higher than they need to be to yield the necessary rate of return on investment at a competitively determined margin, and the adjustment of investment at the extensive and intensive margins is distorted. In terms of the most economical allocation of capital—in terms of genuine conservation—too much investment is directed toward high-cost recovery from oil deposits, and too little investment is directed toward finding and developing new low-cost flowing deposits. The long-run effect must be to price crude oil out of its markets sooner than need be. "Saving" the crude oil at the bottom of legislatively-defined marginal wells is another example of "conservation" devoid of economic content.

The Distinctive Provisions and Conservation

To return to the distinctive tax provisions and their relation to conservation, two general hypothetical cases may be posed: In the first case, let it be assumed that the distinctive tax provisions applying to income from oil and gas production only neutralize the adverse effect on resource allocation of the corporate income tax stemming from the relative riskiness and capital intensity of the oil and

---

greater depths ranging up to 35 barrels a day from a depth of 8,000 feet or more. (Lovejoy, *op. cit.*, p. 34, citing *Revised Civil Statutes of Texas*, Title 102, Article 6049b.)

[104] McKie and McDonald, *op. cit.*, p. 120, citing *Oil and Gas Journal* (Mar. 21, 1960) pp. 100–02.

gas industry.[105] Under ideal[106] state conservation regulations, the distinctive tax provisions would then be thoroughly consistent with genuine conservation. Prices would be distorted neither by tax effects nor by arbitrary restrictions on production rates and practices. They would be free to reflect replacement costs at the margin and to guide producers in their investment decisions at the intensive and extensive margins. Oil and gas would "last" as economic resources as long as they could "pay their own way" in any use. Under present (less than ideal) forms of state regulation, an unsatisfactory time-rate of oil and gas use would prevail, but the fault would lie entirely with the regulations themselves.

In the alternative case, let it be assumed that the distinctive tax provisions applying to income from oil and gas production are not neutral in that they attract resources into the search for and production of oil and gas beyond the point where real economic costs equal real economic returns.[107] Under ideal forms of state conservation regulation, then, oil and gas prices would be artificially lowered and consumption of them would be stimulated. From the point of view of conservation, the time-rate of use of oil and gas would be biased in favor of the present, and the allocation of investment as between the intensive margin and the extensive margin would be biased in favor of the latter. The fault for this violation of genuine conservation, given the specified assumptions, would lie with the distinctive tax provisions. Under present forms of conservation regulation, the results in terms of genuine conservation would be more complex and unspecifiable in the present state of knowledge. Labor and capital would be unduly attracted into the search for oil and gas, but the

---

[105] See pp. 52–57, above.

[106] It is incumbent upon the author to specify what he considers "ideal" forms of state conservation regulation. In general, the following would be considered "ideal":

a. Compulsory unitization of all reservoirs, unit operators being free to adopt spacing patterns and production rates that appear to be in the interest of maximizing the present worth of the underlying deposit.

b. Requirement that purchasers accept and transport tendered oil without discrimination among wells or fields, save on the basis of cost.

c. Restriction of price stabilization activities to just that: the elimination of wide swings in prices resulting from discontinuous major discoveries. Price trends, based on costs at a competitively determined margin, would be allowed to reveal themselves.

[107] As in the Harberger thesis, outlined pp. 49–52 above.

distorted allocation of these resources would not be reflected proportionately in lower prices of oil and gas, greater consumption of them, and an artificially extended margin of exploration. The income benefits of the distinctive tax provisions would be absorbed in part or in whole by the enforced inefficiencies associated with state conservation regulations. Labor and capital would be wasted, but it could not be said that the time-rate of use of oil and gas would in consequence be biased proportionately in favor of the present. It is possible to imagine a case in which, by coincidence, the assumed non-neutral effects of distinctive tax provisions and the effects of state conservation regulations upon the time-rate of use of oil and gas would cancel each other out. Such a situation, if it should occur, could hardly justify the distinctive tax provisions, of course, since their effects under the assumption would still be wasteful. Instead of "subsidizing" the production and consumption of oil and gas, they would instead be "subsidizing" expenditures on unnecessary wells, equipment, and techniques of "saving" natural deposits.

It may be noted, incidentally, that one of the distinctive tax provisions, the expensing of intangible development costs, has a rather direct bearing on the over-drilling problem. In general, this provision reduces the effective cost of development wells. Given the pattern of production allowables attached to spacing of wells, the intangible expensing provision may in some instances provide the marginal incentive for drilling development wells unnecessarily densely.

Conclusion

In conclusion, the effect of distinctive tax provisions on conservation of oil and gas appears to depend on the general resource allocation effects of those provisions in practice. These are highly uncertain. If they are neutral with respect to allocation of resources, they are neutral with respect to conservation also. If not, they finance either a wasteful rate of use of oil and gas or a wasteful system of producing oil and gas.

CHAPTER VI

Considerations of National Security

THE ISSUE OF NATIONAL SECURITY in connection with the tax treatment of income from oil and gas production arises out of the premise that these minerals, particularly oil, are "critical" war materials. Fuels derived from crude oil—gasoline, jet fuel, diesel oil, and fuel oil—are essential to air, naval, and mobile ground forces. In addition, they provide the greater part of the energy consumed in industrial production and civilian transportation. Natural gas, while having relatively little direct use in military operations and civilian transportation, is a fairly close substitute for liquid fuels in stationary installations and thus may be used to free liquid fuels for the uses in which they are essential. The fuel requirements of modern warfare are changing rapidly and are already quite different from those of World War II and the Korean War, in which petroleum products played a strategic role. But it is likely that for some time to come oil and gas will remain essential to certain types of military operations and to production and transporation at home. This is true especially with reference to "limited" wars, and perhaps only slightly less so with reference to nuclear war. On the assumption that in the initial stages of a nuclear war many major industrial centers and rail junctions would be destroyed, air and automotive transportation, both completely dependent on petroleum products for fuel, would assume greater importance than heretofore in linking specialized sectors of the national economy and thus permitting full use of the remaining productive facilities. The discussion to follow is based on such an assumption in the case of nuclear war, although it is recognized that the circumstances of nuclear war might make oil and gas irrelevant to anything but the recovery phase.

Aside from the question of domestic production versus imports of crude oil and products, which is outside the scope of the present study,[108] distinctive tax provisions in the oil and gas industry have some bearing on national security in two possible respects: (1) They may contribute to the creation and maintenance of reserve domestic capacity to produce these critical energy sources. (2) They may contribute to the creation and maintenance of a high enough level of domestic production and consumption of oil and gas that a large volume could be diverted to military uses and war production without seriously encroaching upon absolutely essential civilian uses.

Reserve Capacity

As for the creation and maintenance of *reserve* productive capacity, its value as "war insurance" is rather obvious. True reserve capacity would permit a relatively quick and certain response to sudden large war-time demands. Moreover, geographically widespread reserve capacity would provide some protection against acute shortages resulting from destruction of producing, processing, and transportation facilities in particular localities. The principal question as to the value of reserve capacity to produce crude oil and natural gas is whether there is a similar reserve capacity to transport and process these raw materials. Reserve capacity in crude oil production, for instance, could not supply sudden large war-time demands for gasoline, jet fuel, etc., unless there were a similar reserve capacity in crude oil pipeline and refinery facilities. Moreover, if many of the latter facilities were destroyed in an early-phase nuclear bombing, reserve crude oil capacity would be useless for the dura-

---

[108] This is not to say that import policy is not important in a total scheme of national defense, or that the application of distinctive tax provisions to both foreign and domestic production has no bearing on the relative advantages of imported and domestically produced oil. See p. 7 above for the reasons why international aspects of the subject are disregarded here.

tion of the conflict. While it might be better in principle to have reserve capacity in some phases of production than in none, the point is that reserve capacity in one phase only may be of very limited value.

Divertible domestic capacity implies transportation and processing facilities that match raw material production facilities, but the creation and maintenance of divertible domestic capacity gives rise to problems of its own:

1. There is the question of *permanent* divertibility. If a nation through tax policy or other means deliberately lowers the relative price of a product, use of the product is at first extended into areas in which it is relatively less valuable. Entirely new uses are created, or the product is substituted for some other product in an old use. At first, the policy could be reversed without much difficulty. The new uses would be limited in scope and would not have had time to alter greatly the pattern of production of complementary goods. Producers of substitute products might still have excess capacity with which they could meet restoration of demand. But if the policy of cheapening the product persisted for very long, entirely new patterns of production and consumption, extending to virtually every sector of the economy directly and indirectly, would be formed; the at-first marginal new uses would become "essential" uses, because substitute products with complementary goods would cease to be readily available. What was at first divertible production and consumption would cease to be divertible, the effect becoming stronger in proportion to the passage of time. Thus, a supply of gasoline for personal automobiles is far more essential today than it was during World War II, because suburbanization and shrinkage of public street transportation services, both inextricably related to the relative prices of automobiles and gasoline, now make the use of personal automobiles for getting to work, shopping, and delivering children to school far more necessary for a large portion of the population. Centralization of population and restoration of public street transportation could not be quickly accomplished in an emergency.

2. A policy of artificially cheapening a particular product may lead not only to new uses but also to wasteful applications in old uses, these applications involving complementary goods that cannot

be quickly replaced with others. Thus, for example, relatively cheap gasoline in the United States undoubtedly has contributed to the size and horsepower of automobiles typically in use in this country and hence to the relatively low mileage per gallon of gasoline consumption characteristic of these automobiles. The unnecessary consumption of gasoline per mile[109] of travel could be stopped only by replacing the relatively large and powerful automobiles with the "compact" variety. This would, of course, not be possible in a war emergency.

3. Capacity in use must continually be replaced. A defense policy of trying to maintain divertible capacity raises the question of long-run replacement costs. It is often alleged that the oil and gas industry is now an increasing-cost industry due to growing difficulties of replacing reserves consumed. Whether or not this is in fact true,[110] it is to be expected that at some stage in its life an industry dependent on naturally limited deposits in the crust of the earth *may become* an increasing-cost industry. A policy of lowering the relative price of the product of such an industry with a view to extending the margin of its production and consumption may in the long run be defeated by hastening the day when costs of replacement begin to rise steeply.

4. Artificially lowering the relative price of a particular product necessarily implies artificially raising the relative price of one or more other products. Whatever benefits are derived from lowering one may be offset, in part, in whole, or in excess, by the sacrifices resulting from raising the other. Oil and gas *are* highly important to the nation's security; but they are important for this purpose only in suitable combination with other products. It is by no means certain that a nation can increase the value of the combination by artificially altering the relative prices of components of the combination.

---

[109] Consumption per mile of travel is to be distinguished, of course, from the total miles traveled. The latter may be sharply reduced by means of "car pools" and substitution of other means of transportation, including walking. But where automotive transportation has no close substitute, it makes some difference that past price policy may have been conducive to the production of automotive equipment requiring relatively high inputs of fuel per transportation unit.

[110] See note 85 above.

Effect of Distinctive Tax Provisions
on National Security

It appears, then, that both the reserve-capacity and divertible-capacity approaches to national security have their limitations. Reserve capacity in only one of several mutually dependent industries, or in only one phase of a particular industry, may be quite useless in an emergency. Divertible capacity may in the long run be illusory, and efforts to maintain it for long periods of time may, by inducing wasteful utilization, be positively harmful to national security. However, in certain assumed circumstances, either may be helpful. The question now becomes that of whether and how the distinctive tax provisions applying to income from oil and gas production contribute to creating and maintaining either reserve capacity or divertible capacity in that industry.

EFFECT ON RESERVE CAPACITY. Consider, first, the matter of reserve capacity. The distinctive tax provisions under discussion have the effect of lowering the effective rate of income tax and, other things being equal, attracting a greater volume of productive resources to the search for oil and gas than would be the case with uniform effective income taxation. With competition and no governmental regulation of production, the prices of oil and gas would reflect costs and consumer utility at the margin, and the rate of capacity utilization would tend toward the optimum. Any emergence of excess, or reserve, capacity would set into motion price, investment, and production adjustments that would tend to eliminate it. Thus, with effective competition—and the author believes that the oil and gas industry *is* effectively competitive[111]—the distinctive tax provisions alone could not bring about a persistent state of reserve capacity in the industry.

State production regulation of the type prevailing in the Southwestern states, principally Texas, *can*, at least temporarily, create a general condition of excess capacity in the production of oil and

[111] This opinion, formed independently through observation and analysis, is supported by the conclusion reached by McKie after the most careful and thorough analysis. (McKie, *op. cit.*, p. 571.)

gas. As was explained earlier,[112] this result stems partly from restricting production to estimated "market demand," which tends to support whatever price prevails. It also stems from the exemption of a substantial proportion of wells from any production restriction, these wells being characterized by relatively high costs of production. It is further the result of granting production allowables to the regulated wells largely on the basis of the well-unit itself, without proportionate adjustment for spacing. The result is to gear prices to a legislatively determined margin of recovery and to bring the industry into equilibrium by forcing inefficiencies on properties capable of lower-cost production. These inefficiencies involve, among other things, excess capacity on the part of the properties whose production is kept short of the optimum for efficient recovery.

It is important to emphasize that this sort of excess capacity results from a particular pattern of production regulation and not from the distinctive tax provisions. In the total absence of any distinctive tax provisions, excess capacity would develop from the same pattern of regulation. It is possible, however, that the legislative definition of "marginal" and other exempt wells was conditioned by the existence at the time[113] of the distinctive tax provisions. It is also possible that these provisions, by favoring flush production more than pumped production,[114] increase the degree of excess capacity associated with equilibrium under the present pattern of production regulation. Furthermore, the distinctive tax provisions may make producers in the industry—especially those operating chiefly properties subject to production restraint—more tolerant of the inefficiencies imposed on them by the present system of regulation and thus less inclined to exert themselves to have the system changed. If so, it is likely that oil and gas income tax provisions help create and main-

---

[112] Pp. 80–81 above.

[113] The current statute defining a "marginal" well in Texas was enacted in 1933. (Zimmermann, *op. cit.*, p. 329.) Due to relatively high production costs of marginal wells, percentage depletion is rarely very significant to the operators. It is doubtful, therefore, that the distinctive tax provision had much, if any, bearing upon the legislative definition of a "marginal" well.

[114] Pumped production naturally involves higher costs per unit of production than does flowing production, other things being equal. Higher unit costs of production, in turn, may serve to limit the percentage depletion deduction under the 50-percent-of-net rule.

tain reserve capacity in the industry and to that extent perhaps further the national security. If not, the tax provisions principally determine the level of prices and output at which the excess capacity exists.[115]

A final observation on reserve capacity: Although reserve capacity in the production of oil and gas may be created and maintained by the system of regulation that is typical of the Southwest, aided perhaps by the distinctive tax provisions applying to income from oil and gas production, there is nothing in either the system of regulation or the tax provisions to encourage the creation and maintenance of excess capacity in transportation and refining. Consequently, any national security benefits that may be attributed to the distinctive tax provisions themselves are likely to be modest indeed.

EFFECT ON DIVERTIBLE CAPACITY. Regarding *divertible* domestic capacity in the oil and gas industry, very little more needs to be said. The distinctive tax provisions considered alone tend to create more production and consumption of oil and gas than would take place with equal effective rates of taxation in all industries. In this relative sense, the provisions may contribute to creating and maintaining divertible capacity (with the qualifications about the long run noted above); and to that extent (and with the qualifications mentioned earlier) they may contribute to the national security. Their effects in this direction, however, are limited by the contrary effects of the dominant system of production regulation in the industry. It can only be said that because of the distinctive tax provisions, the system of production regulation has a less adverse effect on the level of production and consumption than it might otherwise.

---

[115] A question may be raised concerning the durability of an excess-capacity equilibrium of the sort just described. Such an equilibrium would be highly durable in a case where the regulatory jurisdiction coincided with the possible area of exploration and production. It would be nondurable to the extent that producers could escape regulation by directing new investments to areas free of the onerous type of regulation. There is some evidence of the migration of oil and gas capital out of Texas (and before the imposition of import quotas, out of the United States) and into those states where production regulation is nonexistent or less conducive to inefficient methods of development and production. If this trend is real and persists for long, it must surely force a change in the system of regulation in Texas and the other "market demand" states.

Conclusion

It therefore appears that the national defense benefits of the distinctive tax provisions applying to income from oil and gas production are highly uncertain, particularly in the long run. The issue is complicated by practices of state regulation of production and the possibility of secular increasing costs of replacement. In view of this uncertainty, the distinctive tax provisions may be less defensible as instruments of national defense than other more direct and certain measures of insuring adequate emergency supplies of oil and gas.[116]

---

[116] There are two rather obvious possibilities, one of which has some historical precedence. First, the federal government may purchase proven reserves from their finders and developers as a part of its program of stockpiling strategic goods. If imports should be increased by a similar amount, the effect would be as if the imported oil were stored in domestic reservoirs for emergency use. The imported oil thus effectively would not compete in the market with domestic production and hence would not "destroy" any part of the domestic industry. Alternatively, the federal government might pay a direct subsidy to the domestic industry for maintaining a given fraction of excess capacity in all phases—production, refining, transportation. Both approaches would be "expensive" in the sense that they would give rise to immediate increases in the federal budget. Socially they might be less expensive, particularly the approach using cheaper foreign oil for a greater part of domestic consumption. Above all, they would be certain. Whatever the cost might be, the government would get what it paid for, and with both costs and benefits laid before them, the taxpayers could decide whether the price were worth paying. Under the present system, even if there are real national defense benefits, there is no way for the taxpayer to link the concealed social costs with those benefits.

CHAPTER VII

Capital Gains Treatment of the Sale of Oil and Gas Properties

THE CAPITAL GAINS TAX, as a special treatment accorded income derived from the sale of capital assets, is, of course, in no sense peculiar to the oil and gas industry. It may, however, have greater actual and potential importance to that industry than to most others. Interests in oil and gas properties are quite easily divided and sold, and pledged interests are regarded as excellent loan collateral. Individual producing properties in the total of properties owned by a company or an individual may be severed from the rest without changing the value of the latter. There is a fairly active market in oil and gas properties, reflecting, in large part, the great diversity of interests of those engaged in the industry. They include, for example, the individual or institutional investor seeking a relatively stable and assured income from proven properties, the major integrated company trying to assure itself of appropriately located sources of refinery runs, the "outsider" who has made a find and developed it but is not interested in managing a productive property, and the wildcatter who would like to "cash in" a discovery in order to finance new ventures. The actual and potential importance of the capital gains tax in the oil and gas industry is enhanced, it is readily seen, by the distinctive provisions allowing the current expensing of the greater portion of finding and development costs. Since the taxpayer is subject to tax on only one-half of a long-term gain on a sale, deductions can be taken for tax savings at a rate in excess of that applying to income taken in the form of proceeds from sale. Finally, there seems to be little or no official restraint on use of the capital gains device for converting income in the oil and gas industry. Gains arising out of the sale of assets that in the ordinary course of business are regularly offered for sale to customers cannot by law be considered "capital gains."[117] Although oil and gas deposits would seem to fall in this category, in actual practice capital gains treatment is allowed in nearly all cases of sales of oil and gas property interests.[118]

Value of Capital Gains Alternative

For the ordinary firm in the industry, regularly engaged in finding and producing oil and gas, the capital gains feature in the tax laws is potentially of value because it enhances the relative attractiveness of selling individual properties or liquidating the firm[119] rather than continuing to produce oil and gas for sale. Thus, the possibility of loss arising out of adverse influences on regular income that would not be fully shared by a purchaser is reduced by virtue of the capital gains alternative. For example, a firm that has been growing rapidly in the past, drilling increasing numbers of wells and charging off most of their cost as operating expense, may find its further growth possibilities reduced and its prospective income tax liability sharply increased because of smaller prospective deductions for capital consumption. It can avoid a "catch-up" of deferred income tax liability by selling out and taking capital gains treatment on the proceeds. The attractiveness of this alternative would of course depend on the realizable proceeds from sale and the available rate of return on the best alternative investment,

[117] Lawrence H. Seltzer, *The Nature and Treatment of Capital Gains and Losses* (National Bureau of Economic Research; Princeton University Press, 1951), p. 3. See also U. S. Congress, Joint Economic Committee, *The Federal Revenue System: Facts and Problems, 1961* (Government Printing Office, 1961), pp. 49–59, for a summary of the current status of capital gains taxation in the United States, including special provisions applying to designated types of transactions.

[118] There appears to be some uncertainty still about the treatment of gains from the sale of "in-oil" payments, which bear some resemblance to royalties. For a discussion of this point, see Joint Economic Committee, *The Federal Revenue System*, pp. 55–56.

[119] When a firm sells all its assets and is liquidated, a capital gains tax liability is created for the stockholders only; the corporation, as such, incurs no tax liability.

adjusted for difference in risk. The possibility of deriving proceeds from sale in excess of present worth to the firm at any given rate of discount is increased by the fact that the buyer may use the purchase price as the basis of cost depletion, with resulting capital consumption deductions larger than those possible at the maximum rate of percentage depletion.

The capital gains alternative is potentially of value also because of the possibility of changes in the distinctive tax provisions applying to the industry, particularly reduction of the rate, or elimination, of percentage depletion. In cases where selling for capital gains is nearly as attractive as operating with percentage depletion, a reduction in the rate, or elimination, of the latter would induce sales. The sellers would avoid some part of the higher income tax payments they would have had to make, and the buyers would also avoid income tax payments at higher rates by using the purchase price as the basis of cost depletion. The actual increase in long-run Treasury receipts in consequence of the change would depend on how closely substitutable capital gains advantages are for percentage depletion advantages.[120]

Some simple examples will illustrate these points. They are realistic enough both to support the generalizations and to suggest the kinds of circumstances in which the capital gains alternative would be chosen by an oil and gas producer. Assume a fully developed oil property expected to produce a constant number of barrels per year for ten years.[121] The price per barrel at the wellhead is expected to be constant at $3.00, with operating costs constant at $0.80 per barrel.[122] For simplicity, it is assumed that there are no deductions for capital consumption other than for depletion—

[120] It may be noted incidentally that selling for capital gains as a reaction to reduction of the benefits of current distinctive tax provisions might lead to a significantly higher degree of concentration in the industry.

[121] Most oil properties have a longer life than ten years, even after full development, and production per year tends to diminish over the period of productive life. The assumed life of ten years is a mathematically convenient one, and it does not materially affect the realism of the *comparison of alternatives* made below. Production regulation tends to flatten the normal downward-sloping curve of production, so the assumption of constant annual production, also made as a matter of mathematical convenience, is not entirely unrealistic. Although these assumptions are acceptable for the purposes at hand, the resulting present values should not be interpreted as currently typical for the industry.

[122] The author believes these to be reasonably realistic values for recent years.

either percentage or cost depletion.[123] The nominal income tax rate is assumed to be 50 percent, and the effective rate on long-term capital gains 25 percent. Future production, prices, and costs are regarded as sufficiently certain to justify a rate of discount of future cash flow of 8 percent, both to the owner of the fully developed property and to a prospective buyer of the property. All present values are computed on the basis of one barrel of net working interest.[124]

Computation of the present value of this property per barrel of net working interest to the lessee-operator using percentage depletion is shown below:

A

$3.00 price per barrel
  .80 operating costs
  _____
 2.20 cash flow before allowance for income taxes
  .82 percentage depletion (27½% of gross)
  _____
 1.38 taxable income
  .69 income tax at 50%
  _____
 1.51 net cash flow after tax (2.20−.69)

Present value of a dollar spread over ten years in equal amounts, discounted at 8% a year: $0.671
Present value of property per barrel of net working interest = $0.671 (1.51)
= $1.01

If the lessee-operator had an alternative use for capital which, after allowance for difference in risk, would yield him, say, 15 percent, the real economic value to him of the oil-producing property would reflect that higher rate of discount. Computation of that value is:

B

Present value of a dollar spread over ten years in equal amounts, discounted at 15% a year: $0.502
Present value of property per barrel of net working interest = $0.502 (1.51)
= $0.76

[123] The exclusion of depreciation on tangible investment is purely a matter of simplification. Since both buyer and seller would have to follow the same procedures in depreciating tangible equipment, and since depreciation allowances are not a variable in the examples, the comparison of alternatives is in no way affected by this omission.

[124] The net working interest is the share of the lessee in the underlying reserves, i.e., gross recoverable reserves less royalty. Computation on this basis permits elimination of the royalty as a cost to the producer, hence as a factor in determining present worth.

If percentage depletion were eliminated, the lessee-operator would have to confine his depletion deductions to his capitalized cost basis, here assumed to be 2 percent of gross income,[125] or $0.06 per barrel of production. Without percentage depletion, then, the computation of present value per barrel of net working interest would be:

C

$3.00 price per barrel
.80 operating costs
_____
2.20 cash flow before allowance for income tax
.06 cost depletion
_____
2.14 taxable income
1.07 income tax at 50%

1.13 net cash flow after income tax (2.20 − 1.07)

Present value of a dollar spread over ten years in equal amounts, discounted at 8% a year: $0.671
Present value of property per barrel of net working interest = $0.671 (1.13)
= $0.76

To a prospective buyer of the property willing to discount future income at 8 percent, the present value of a dollar of net cash flow would be exactly the same as to the lessee-operator using the same rate of discount. At this rate of discount, however, the buyer would find it in his interest to use cost depletion based on the purchase price. This, together with the purchase price, can be shown as follows:

D

Present value of a dollar spread over ten years in equal amounts, discounted at 8% a year: $0.671
Present value of property per barrel of net working interest
= .671 (net cash flow before tax minus income tax)
= .671 [2.20 − .5(2.20 − present value)]
= .671 (1.10 + .5 present value)
= $1.11

Whereas the deduction for depletion using percentage depletion would be only $0.82, the deduction using cost depletion would be $1.11.

If the lessee-operator sold the property for $1.11 per barrel of net working interest, having a remaining cost basis of $0.06 per

<hr>

[125] See note 16 above.

barrel, he would have to pay a capital gains tax of .25 (1.11 − .06) = $0.26 per barrel. His net proceeds then would be $1.11 − 0.26 = $0.85. This is a smaller amount than the worth to him of retaining the property and using percentage depletion, assuming his capital is worth only 8 percent to him. Presumably, in this case, no sale could be effected. But if the lessee-operator could use his capital for some other purpose and earn 15 percent on it, he could make a real economic profit of $0.09 per barrel of net working interest by selling out. He would sacrifice the present worth of $0.76 per barrel (discounted at 15 percent) in exchange for net proceeds of $0.85 per barrel. In such a case, as with an experienced wildcatter needing funds to carry out a promising new venture or an owner of a new discovery needing funds to develop it, the sale presumably would be effected to the benefit of both parties.[126] Similarly, if percentage depletion were eliminated, the lessee-operator would profit by selling out for capital gains, even though he could earn no more on his proceeds than the purchaser (8 percent). By coincidence in the example, the real economic profit to the seller would again be $0.09 per barrel of net working interest ($0.85 − 0.76).

It is interesting to note the financial position of the Treasury with respect to the property in question. With the lessee-operator retaining the property and using percentage depletion, the Treasury receives $0.69 per barrel of net working interest spread over ten years. Discounted at 4 percent a year, the Treasury's approximate long-term borrowing cost, such receipts have a present worth of $0.56 per barrel. If percentage depletion were eliminated, the lessee-operator's income tax liability would be increased to $1.07 per barrel, with a present worth to the Treasury of $0.87 per barrel. Without a sale for capital gains, then, the Treasury might expect to gain discounted receipts worth $0.31 per barrel of net working interest. With the sale, however, the Treasury would immediately receive $0.26 per barrel as the capital gains tax and then $0.52 per barrel from the purchaser-operator [.5(2.20 − 1.11)] spread over ten years. The present worth at 4 percent of these receipts would be $0.68 per barrel, representing a gain over the percentage deple-

---

[126] It may be observed that much the same gain could be realized if the lessee-operator could borrow an amount equal to three-fourths the value of his property at 8 percent interest. Of course, there would be a restraint on a borrower arising from the necessity to make regular provision for repayment.

tion case of $0.12 per barrel. With a sale for capital gains, the Treasury's income from the property in question would be increased in consequence of elimination of percentage depletion, but by $0.19 less (in present worth per barrel of net working interest) than if the capital gains alternative were not available to the lessee-operator.

The effect of the capital gains alternative for the royalty owner, which is outside the scope of this study, can easily be worked out using whatever assumptions seem appropriate as to cost basis of the royalty owner and respective marginal tax rates of buyer and seller.

The ABC Deal

The "ABC deal,"[127] a device that has become rather widespread in the oil and gas industry in recent years, may be used to enhance the value of the capital gains alternative by giving a buyer a somewhat better depletion position, the financial advantages of which he may share with the seller in the form of a higher purchase price. In an ABC deal, A is the seller of a producing property. He sells the property to B for a stipulated price, accepting a partial payment in cash from B and retaining an oil payment in settlement for the balance. The oil payment A then sells to C, an investor. A takes capital gains on the cash transactions with B and C, the amount received in the two transactions totaling the stipulated selling price of the property. B and C now own the total rights to production, and on their respective interests each will take the higher of cost or percentage depletion. C almost always will take cost depletion, since he has no production costs to bear and the 50-percent-of-net limitation usually in such a case causes allowable percentage depletion to be less than allowable cost depletion. B, however, may be able to take percentage depletion, either from the beginning or after the oil payment is liquidated. If so, the total depletion taken by B and C together will exceed that which B alone would have taken had he purchased the property for cash and taken cost depletion over its life, as he almost certainly would have done.

[127] The ABC deal is elaborately explained in both its legal and its economic aspects in J. Henry Wilkinson, Jr., "ABC—From A to Z," *Texas Law Review*, Vol. 38 (June 1960), pp. 673–724; and J. Henry Wilkinson, Jr., "ABC Transactions and Related Income Tax Plans," *Texas Law Review*, Vol. 40 (November 1961), pp. 18–87.

Even if B takes only cost depletion, moreover, there is an advantage to him in the ABC deal in that he effectively accelerates the deductions from his gross income for tax purposes. Both the possibility that B can take percentage depletion at some time and the effective acceleration of B's total tax return deductions stem from the tax treatment of the oil payment from B's point of view. Under the terms of the payment, he is obliged to turn over to the owner of the payment (now C) a stipulated fraction of the value of the production from the property when and as it occurs, each payment being credited against the principal amount of the oil payment (and accrued interest on the balance outstanding). The principal amount of the oil payment is equally excludable for tax purposes from both B's gross income and his cost basis. Since his cost basis is reduced by a greater *percentage* than his gross income, percentage depletion may provide a larger deduction than cost depletion, despite the 50-percent-of-net limitation. But even if B finds that cost depletion will give him the larger deduction, the exclusion of the oil payment from his cost basis has the effect of accelerating his cost depletion deductions in time and increasing the value of his tax savings from such deductions. He is thus in a position to offer a somewhat better price to A than if he had to buy outright for cash.

Effect on Outsiders

Discussion of the capital gains alternative in connection with the distinctive tax provisions applying to income from oil and gas production would not be complete without reference to the case of "outsiders" with other sources of income who engage in the search for oil and gas. Assume a person, or syndicate of persons, with large enough personal income to be in the 90 percent marginal bracket. Such a person or persons can engage in the search for oil and gas and charge off unsuccessful outlays against personal income tax liability, involving a net cost, under the assumptions, of ten cents on the dollar. Any discoveries can be developed for relatively low net costs, since intangible development costs, amounting to perhaps 80 percent of total development costs, may likewise be charged to other personal income. Then, with a very low cost basis remaining in the fully developed property, the finder-developers can sell it to, say, an integrated company for capital gains. They charge off nearly all of the costs at a 90 percent tax rate and pay 25 percent on the net proceeds from sale. Of course, they must find some oil and/or gas to make a profit, but it is easy to see that they need not find as much to make it profitable to them as if the capital gains alternative were not available, or if all finding and development costs had to be capitalized and used as the cost basis of either depletion or gains from sale of capital assets. Given the present structure of personal income tax rates in this country, it is not surprising, then, that in recent years rather large sums are believed to have been expended by "outsiders" on finding oil and gas and developing discoveries.[128]

Entirely without reference to percentage depletion, the expensing of capital outlays in combination with the capital gains feature in the tax laws acts as a powerful attraction to capital and must be presumed to affect the allocation of capital among industries. In the present state of knowledge about the value of capital involved and the relevant underlying personal tax rates, it is impossible to judge how much, if any, misallocation of resources results

Conclusion

The capital gains feature thus enhances the value of those distinctive tax provisions in the oil and gas industry that permit the expensing of certain capital outlays. It permits a firm that can find a willing buyer to escape forever some[129] of the taxes saved through prior expensing of finding and development costs. Moreover, it would permit such firms to escape the full consequences of a reduction in percentage depletion and would limit the Treasury's financial gains from such a reduction. It is impossible, then, to evaluate fully the distinctive tax provisions or to predict the results of any change in them without reference to the capital gains alternative and the circumstances under which it is, or may be, used.

[128] There are no official estimates of how much "outside" money is invested in the oil and gas industry. From conversations with members of the industry who have some "feel" of the matter, the author has gained the impression that the amounts may run to several hundred million dollars annually. It should be emphasized, however, that no direct evidence is available to support this impression.

[129] If the taxpayer's deferred liabilities should be allowed to "catch up" with him, he would have to pay them at the rate applying to ordinary income. By selling out, he effectively pays off these deferred liabilities at the lower capital gains rate.

CHAPTER VIII

Price Effects of Changing Percentage Depletion

THERE IS NO SERIOUS CURRENT PROPOSAL that the rate of percentage depletion applying to income from oil and gas production be increased. If any change takes place in the near future, it is almost certain to be a reduction. Accordingly, the following discussion will be confined to the probable price effects of a reduction in the rate of percentage depletion and, to take the most extreme case, it will be assumed that percentage depletion is eliminated altogether. It will further be assumed that the other distinctive tax provisions remain unchanged.

Immediate Effects

The immediate effect of eliminating percentage depletion would be, of course, to increase the current income tax liability of operating firms in the industry and of others (e.g., royalty owners) having direct interests in oil and gas production. Assuming a typical marginal income tax rate of 50 percent for operating firms, the increase in income tax liability of such firms would be one-half of the former excess of percentage depletion over cost basis. This increase in turn would influence managerial decisions regarding production and investment through two different effects, which may be identified as the liquidity effect and the incentive effect.[130] The former is the effect of change in the availability of funds to finance current operations and investments, and the latter is the effect of change in prospective earnings after tax from future production. Both effects would be negative if percentage depletion were eliminated and presumably would discourage investments in finding and proving new oil and gas deposits. The rate of growth of producing capacity consequently would tend to decline relative to the rate of growth of demand for oil and gas, and, other things being equal, the prices of oil and gas would tend to rise both absolutely and relatively. As will be explained below, however, there are several qualifications to this generalization conveniently impounded in "other things being equal."

The existing system of production regulation, i.e., restriction of production to "reasonable market demand," under the conservation laws of most of the major producing states would, if anything, assist in the upward adjustment of prices. Where there is particular solicitude for the welfare of the marginal producer, as in Texas, an increase in prices following elimination of percentage depletion would be regarded by the regulatory authorities as desirable; and it may be assumed that production allowables would be managed so as to support an increase in prices. If major buyer-producers should immediately post higher prices and the quantities of oil and gas demanded should consequently be decreased, adjustment of production to "market demand" would provide support for the higher level of prices. In the nature of the system, production thereafter would be allowed to increase no more rapidly than demand; hence the initially higher prices, if maintained by major buyer-producers, would continue to be supported by the regulatory system.

Liquidity Effect

It may be helpful to assess in quantitative terms the impact of eliminating percentage depletion in oil and gas production. Consider, first, the liquidity effect. In 1960, the gross value of oil and gas production in the United States was as follows:[131]

---

[130] The expressions are borrowed from Steiner, *op. cit.*, p. 954.

[131] Bureau of Mines, *Minerals Yearbook*, Vol. 2 (1960), p. 6. The well-head value of natural gas converted to natural gas liquids is included in the natural gas total.

Natural gas: 12.77 trillion cu. ft. at $0.14/thous. cu. ft. = $1,790 million
Crude petroleum: 2,575 million bbls. at $2.88/bbl.   = 7,419 million
                                                     _____
                                    Total   = $9,209 million

After allowance for an estimated average royalty of 14 percent,[132] the net working interest value of oil and gas production was $7,920 million. Assuming an average excess of allowable depletion over cost basis of 20 percent, the increased income tax liability of operating interests resulting from the elimination of percentage depletion would be:

.50[.20($7,920 million)] = $792 million.

The significance of this sum is indicated by the fact that it is about 15 percent of total exploration and development outlays of the domestic industry in recent years.[133] To put it another way, the sum would finance the drilling and equipping of about 15,000 wells of average depth with typical distribution among oil wells, gas wells, service wells, and dry holes,[134] or almost one-third of the total of approximately 47,000 wells drilled in the United States in 1960.[135]

Incentive Effect

As for the initial incentive effect, an approximation can be made in this way: Assume that the excess of allowable depletion over

[132] The usual landowner's royalty is 12.5 percent (one-eighth), but, particularly on public lands, a royalty of 16.7 percent (one-sixth) is becoming more common. Overriding royalties also add to the average royalty percentage paid by operating interests. The 14 percent used here is believed to be reasonably representative.

[133] Outlays for exploration and development in 1959 were estimated to be $5.3 billion. (American Petroleum Institute, Independent Petroleum Association of America, and Mid-Continent Oil and Gas Association, *Joint Association Survey: Estimated Expenditures and Receipts of U. S. Oil and Gas Producing Industry,* [1959], p. 2.)

[134] The calculation is based on an estimated average cost per well of $53,000. The 1958 Census of Mineral Industries indicates an average cost of $51,600 per well in 1958. (Bureau of the Census, *1958 Census of Mineral Industries, Industry and Product Reports: Crude Petroleum and Natural Gas* [June 1960], p. 17.) The Joint Association Survey of 1959 reports an average cost of drilling and equipping wells (excluding service wells) in 1959 of $53,500. (American Petroleum Institute, Independent Petroleum Association of America, and Mid-Continent Oil and Gas Association, *Joint Association Survey of Industry Drilling Costs* [1959], p. 3.)

[135] *Oil and Gas Journal* (Annual Review Issue, 1961). The matter is expressed in this way merely to indicate the relative magnitude of $792 million in the oil and gas industry. It is not suggested that drilling *per se* would bear the full burden of reduced liquidity; nor is it suggested that any reduction in drilling would necessarily be "across the board" with respect to exploration and development.

cost basis is 20 percent of gross income, that the rate of capital turnover in the oil and gas industry is 0.90 a year, and that the rate of
return on equity capital averages, before elimination of percentage
depletion, 24 percent.[136] The rate of return on sales (gross income)
would be 24 ÷ .90, or approximately 27 percent. Eliminating percentage depletion would, assuming a 50-percent marginal income
tax rate, reduce net income after taxes by one-half the net depletion
benefit, or by 10 percent of gross income. The margin on sales
would consequently fall to 17 percent (27 percent − 10 percent),
and the rate of return on equity would fall to about 15 percent
(17 percent × .90). Thus, the reduction in rate of return immediately resulting from the elimination of percentage depletion under
the assumptions given would be from 24 percent to 15 percent, a
decrease of more than one-third. The relative decrease would of
course be greater at lower initial rates of return. For instance, if the
initial rate of return were only 18 percent, the reduction would be
to 9 percent, or one-half. With an initial rate of return of 9 percent,
eliminating percentage depletion would, in its first impact, wipe
out net income altogether. A distinction must be made between
the *prospective* rate of return on new investments and the *realized* rate
of return on existing investments, but the above calculation is
indicative of what would happen to the prospective rate of return
if no cost and price adjustments in future could be assumed.

Longer-run Effects

The foregoing suggests that the impact of eliminating percentage depletion would be great enough to induce a sharp reduction
in the oil and gas industry's outlays for finding and developing
new oil and gas deposits, and hence to have some material effect
on the level of oil and gas prices. It seems reasonable to believe
that prices would be affected almost at once, partly reflecting

[136] The rates used here coincide approximately with those calculated by the author
from IRS data reflecting income tax returns of corporations classified as producers of
crude petroleum, natural gas, and natural gasoline in the years 1949–51 and 1953–56.
See the qualifications to these findings in Appendix A, page 144. The representativeness
of the rates need not be at issue here, since the present purpose is to suggest the possible
magnitude of incentive effects within the limits of a reasonable range of possible rates
of return in the industry. See the results of assuming lower rates of return below.

anticipations of more restricted capacity and higher prices in future. There would be some speculative premium on withholding current production, at least to the extent of slowing down the rate of development of known deposits. With continued growth of demand relative to capacity, initially existing excess capacity would gradually be eliminated, and further increases in prices would be feasible. Eventually—and the process might require several years for completion—price increases combined with any cost reductions that might accompany the adjustment would restore profit margins to the level that would be consistent with a rate of growth of capacity equal to the rate of growth of demand. After that time, there would be no further price changes as a direct result of eliminating percentage depletion.

How high would prices rise? It is impossible to answer that question precisely because the size of the price adjustment would depend largely on the unpredictable accompanying cost adjustments to be discussed below. It *is* possible, however, to estimate an upper limit. Assume no reductions in unit costs, and assume that the initial profit margin must be restored to re-achieve equilibrium. Again using an assumed excess of allowable depletion over cost basis of 20 percent of gross income and a 50 percent marginal rate of income tax, the necessary increase in price would be 20 percent. The loss of net income through elimination of percentage depletion is 50 percent of the previous net depletion benefit. If an amount equal to the previous net depletion benefit is added to the profit margin before tax, the loss can be offset. [137] The example shown on the following page, using round numbers for convenience, illustrates the point.

In the light of this upper limit, it is now possible more closely to approximate the amount of the price increase that would tend to occur in response to eliminating percentage depletion by asking

[137] To generalize,

$$p = \frac{dt}{1 - t}$$

where:

p = percentage increase in price,
d = net depletion benefit as percent of initial price,
t = marginal income tax rate.

the question, What forces would operate to impede or limit a price increase?

	With percentage depletion	Without percentage depletion
	(amounts per barrel)	
Price	$3.00	$3.60
Explicit costs	−1.40	−1.40
Excess percentage depletion over cost basis	− .60	
Taxable income	1.00	2.20
Income tax at 50%	− .50	−1.10
Add back net depletion benefit	+ .60	
Net after taxes	1.10	1.10

Elasticity of Demand for Gas and Oil

On the demand side, there is the question of the price elasticity of demand for oil and gas. The more elastic the demand for oil and gas, the more difficult and time-consuming it would be to raise the level of prices and the greater would be the burden on production and cost adjustments in the process of restoring profit margins. There appear to be no quantitative estimates of the price elasticity of demand for either crude oil or natural gas.[138] It is the general opinion, however, that the price elasticity of demand for these two minerals is quite low, well below unity but above zero. An analysis of the factors affecting the price elasticity of demand for oil and gas lends logical support to this opinion.

Consider first the availability to buyers of oil and gas of the alternative of turning to lower-cost foreign sources of supply. Given the existing difference between foreign and domestic costs, in a free and open world market any effort to raise domestic prices would only increase imports. Similarly, with a protective tariff fixed in terms of cents per barrel or a percentage of the import price, a rise

[138] Zimmermann (*op. cit.*, p. 86, note 53) refers to an unidentified study conducted some years ago that put the price elasticity of demand for gasoline at .13. Since gasoline accounts for about 45 percent of the yield of crude petroleum, this figure suggests the general size of the price elasticity of demand for petroleum. Allowing for a probably higher elasticity of demand for other petroleum products and some rigidity in product proportions, it seems to the author that the elasticity of demand for petroleum probably is not greater than, say, .30.

in domestic prices would tend to increase imports. But under the current system of import quotas in the United States, the import alternative is severely limited, and the price elasticity of demand for oil and gas is almost entirely a question of the availability of domestic substitute commodities.

As for closely substitutable commodities at home, gas is now quite competitive with coal in certain uses, particularly in fueling electric power generating plants. A rise in the *relative* price of gas would adversely affect its sales in such uses. For other uses, however, such as in home heating and the manufacture of plastics and petrochemicals, gas now has little or no competition from coal or other commodities. The closest substitute for crude petroleum is shale oil, since coal now offers no remotely feasible alternative as a commercial source of motor and jet fuels. There remains some oil-coal competition in the fueling of industrial and utility power plants, but this market is a minor part of the total market of the petroleum industry. The full costs of shale oil extraction at the present time appear to place that commodity well outside the margin of commercial feasibility. A substantial rise in the *relative* price of crude oil, perhaps as much as 10 or 20 percent, could probably take place before there would be a significant threat from shale oil. Such a rise in the *relative* price of crude oil would be a most unlikely result of eliminating percentage depletion, particularly if it were eliminated for all minerals at once.[139] In the very long run, an increase in the prices of gasoline, fuel oil, natural gas, and other products of the industry undoubtedly would induce fuel-saving innovations in the equipment using these products. Even allowing for this effect, however, it seems reasonable to conclude that the price elasticity of demand for domestically produced oil and gas would offer little impediment to the necessary upward adjustment of oil and gas prices in response to the elimination of percentage depletion.

[139] Since the rate of percentage depletion for oil and gas is higher than that for shale oil and coal (10 percent), elimination of percentage depletion in all mineral industries would probably tend to increase the relative price of oil and gas. However, the effect would not necessarily be proportionate to the nominal rates, for two reasons. First, the proportionate size of cost basis would vary among industries. Second, in some of the mineral industries, including coal and shale, the base of percentage depletion is a price that reflects considerable transportation and processing. The nominal rates are thus not directly comparable. (See John H. Lichtblau and Dillard P. Spriggs, *The Oil Depletion Issue* [Petroleum Industry Research Foundation, 1959], p. 46, for a short discussion of the depletion base for minerals other than oil and gas.)

Supply and Cost Factors

On the supply or cost side there are several factors which would operate to limit the increase in oil and gas prices that would tend to occur in response to an elimination of percentage depletion. First, as is well known, there is at the present time great excess capacity in the oil and gas industry, particularly in crude petroleum production.[140] An increase in demand relative to productive capacity would tend to lower unit costs up to the neighborhood of maximum efficient rates of recovery, thus tending to restore profit margins without price increases. In the Southwestern states, where nearly all of the excess capacity exists, demand could grow relative to capacity for some time before encountering increasing costs of supply. Not enough about existing cost functions is known for an estimate to be made of the possible saving in cost to be made by expanding output relative to capacity in the Southwestern states, but the possibility of some such cost saving is beyond doubt.

A rough idea of the possibilities of adjusting to the elimination of percentage depletion through cost-saving expansion of capacity utilization can be conveyed by means of the following example: Assume a crude oil price of $3.00/bbl., incremental production costs (with excess capacity) of $0.50/bbl., and a marginal tax rate of 50 percent. Each incremental barrel of *working interest* production would add $1.25 to the industry's net income [.50(3.00 − .50)]. It would require an additional gross production of about 740 million barrels a year, or about two million barrels a day, to replace, at this rate, the estimated impact loss of $792 million from eliminating percentage depletion. Texas alone could absorb that expansion of production and still have 0.3 million barrels a day of excess capacity. Such an expansion would absorb less than two-thirds of the nation's total excess capacity as of the present time.[141]

Second, as indicated in a previous section, most oil fields in the United States have been, and are being, developed with wastefully

[140] As of January 1, 1960, the National Petroleum Council estimated a total productive capacity in the United States of approximately 10.6 million barrels a day. Actual U. S. production for 1960 was just over 7 million barrels a day, indicating an excess capacity of 3.6 million barrels a day, or 50 percent of actual production. Of the total national excess capacity, 2.3 million barrels a day, or more than two-thirds, existed in the state of Texas alone. (Production data from Bureau of Mines, *Minerals Yearbook*, Vol. 2 [1960], p. 6.)

[141] See note 140 above.

dense spacing patterns. There is little to be done about the existing fields, and there is nothing in the elimination of percentage depletion that would necessarily force a more rational development of new fields. Nonetheless, the industry is already growing restive over the proven waste involved in excessively dense spacing, and the pressures on profit margins that would result from elimination of percentage depletion might well provide the final incentive needed to force upon the regulatory authorities a new and cost-saving approach to spacing. Any improvement in this regard at all would ease the industry's adjustment to elimination of percentage depletion.

Finally, on new leases arranged after the elimination of percentage depletion, oil and gas firms could—and undoubtedly would—reduce costs by paying smaller lease bonuses and conceivably smaller royalties. Given oil and gas prospects would then be worth less to such firms, and the liquidity squeeze associated with the first impact would limit funds available for new lease commitments. Over a very long period, perhaps in the range of ten to fifteen years, oil and gas operators might shift backward to landowners much of the burden of any increase in their income tax liabilities. Lease bonuses and royalties are largely pure economic rent, a type of income that can be reduced without affecting the supply of actual and potential oil and gas deposits accessible to operating interests.[142] Since the search for, and production of, oil and gas does not interfere greatly with the other land uses, landowners would have a relatively low reservation price in the lease-royalty bargain. Until that price was reached, operators could freely pass back to supramarginal landowners the burden of additional taxes, but only through contracts made subsequent to the increase in tax liability. Since it would require such a long time to run off existing contracts and replace them with new ones, the cost saving available to operators through this means would be quite limited in the short run. Nonetheless, such cost saving of this nature as could be achieved in the short run would facilitate adjust-

---

[142] The lease bonus is legally regarded as an advance royalty. The mineral royalty differs from Ricardian land rent in the traditional sense in that the source of the royalty is exhaustible. The economic significance of the royalty is, however, identical with that of land rent: both are price-determined rather than price-determining, and neither is socially necessary to call forth a productive service by the landowner.

ment to the elimination of percentage depletion without a proportionate increase in oil and gas prices.[143]

Conclusion

In view of the cost reductions that would come with adjustment to the elimination of percentage depletion it seems likely that the long-run price increases necessary might be closer to zero than to the upper limit of 20 percent. It should be emphasized, however, that this conclusion rests to a considerable extent on the present existence of great excess capacity in the industry and of substantial room for reducing the costs of oil field development through wider spacing. Cost reductions through spacing reforms and elimination of existing excess capacity would require new legislation at the state level and specifically permissive behavior on the part of regulatory officials. While eliminating or reducing the distinctive tax provisions would probably provide strong motivation for the indicated official actions, it would by no means assure them. The special case envisioned here, involving substantial excess capacity at a particular point in time, is not necessarily in conflict with the general case discussed in Chapter III above, involving initial equilibrium in the industry and abstracting from regulatory forms, on the basis of which it was argued that the corporation income tax without the distinctive provisions would tend to produce a significant increase in the relative price of oil and gas. It should also be emphasized that full adjustment of the industry to the elimination of the distinctive tax provisions might require several years, during which the process of accommodation would be painful indeed. The longer the required period of adjustment and the more painful the process, the more likely is some unforeseen development—including some sort of meliorative governmental intervention—that would alter the above conclusions with respect to the long run.

[143] Since this was written, Paul Davidson has independently published a similar argument as to the incidence of the additional tax burden created by the elimination of percentage depletion. ("Policy Problems of the Crude Oil Industry," *American Economic Review*, Vol. 53 [March 1963], pp. 101–07.) The author does not agree, however, with Davidson's conclusion that percentage depletion could be eliminated without significantly shifting the margin of exploration. This conclusion depends on the unwarranted assumption that all prospective oil lands on which lease bonus and royalty bids might be made are supramarginal at least to the extent of the net tax benefits of percentage depletion.

CHAPTER IX

Revenue Effects of Changing Percentage Depletion

As IN THE PREVIOUS CHAPTER, the discussion here will be based on the assumed elimination of percentage depletion altogether. However, estimates of revenue effects will be confined to those relevant to the domestic oil and gas industry. A reasonably accurate estimate of revenue effects would involve a complete analysis of input-output relations in the economy, an estimate of all supply and demand elasticities, and a prediction of the probable incidence of any net change in the total tax burden. Needless to say, all that can be attempted here is a very crude first approximation; and, for reasons that will later become apparent, that approximation must rest upon some arbitrary assumptions.

Initial Impact

A good place to begin is with the apparent impact effect of elimination of percentage depletion. In a letter to Senator Harry F. Byrd of May 6, 1958, Dan Throop Smith, then Deputy Secretary of the Treasury, estimated that elimination of percentage depletion in the domestic oil and gas industry would mean an increase in gross revenue to the United States Treasury of $925 million per year. After allowing for a consequent reduction of $150 million a year in taxes on personal income from dividends, the estimated net revenue increase was $775 million per year.[144] The estimate reflected no allowance for any change in production and prices that might take place in consequence of the elimination of percentage depletion.[145]

Information on average effective tax rates, average effective depletion rates, average dividend payout rates, etc., in the domestic oil and gas industry is not readily available. However, with certain simple assumptions Professor Smith's results have been closely approximated for this study, the oil and gas production and price data used being those for 1957. In addition, a more up-to-date estimate has been made, based on data for 1960. The calculations and results are given below:

As indicated earlier, the gross value of oil and gas production in the United States in 1960 was $9,209 million, $1,289 million representing royalty interests and $7,920 million operating interests.[146] Assume for both royalty owners and operating interests an average excess of allowable depletion over cost basis of 20 percent of gross income.[147] The net depletion deduction of royalty owners would be $259 million, and at an average effective marginal tax rate of 30 percent the net depletion benefit to royalty owners would be $77 million. The net depletion deduction of operating interests would be $1,584 million, and at an average effective marginal tax rate of 50 percent the net tax saving to operating interests would be $792 million. The sum of the gross tax benefits is $869 million.[148] Smith estimated an adverse dividend effect of about 16 percent of the gross tax benefit. Using a similar percentage, we get a figure of $139 million as the adverse dividend effect for 1960, leaving an estimated net revenue gain of $730 million. To repeat, such an

[144] The letter was introduced into the *Congressional Record* (Senate) Vol. 104 (Aug. 11, 1958), pp. 15,536–37, by Senator Paul H. Douglas. See also Steiner, *op. cit.*, p. 951, for a reproduction of the revenue estimate.

[145] Letter from Deputy Secretary Dan Throop Smith to Senator Harry F. Byrd of May 6, 1958. See citation in note 144.

[146] See p. 103.

[147] It should be remembered that royalties may be purchased, either *per se* or as general mineral rights in land, thus creating a cost basis for the owners.

[148] It will be noted that this figure is smaller than that estimated by Smith on the basis of earlier (presumably 1956 or 1957) data. At least part of the explanation is a decline from 1957 to 1960 in both prices and production of crude petroleum, a decline not fully offset by increases in production and prices of natural gas in the same period.

estimate is of the impact effect only. Put another way, it implicitly assumes no change in production and prices because of elimination of percentage depletion.

Effect on Taxable Profit Margin

In the previous chapter, it was argued that elimination of percentage depletion would at once set into motion investment (and possibly production) effects that would tend to increase prices and/or reduce unit costs. These effects would lead to an eventual new equilibrium in which initial profit margins after taxes would be restored. On a per barrel basis, the before-tax profit margin in the new equilibrium would be larger than it was initially by the amount of the previous excess of percentage depletion over cost basis. The *taxable* margin is thus increased by an amount twice that of the previous net depletion deduction—once for the elimination of the deduction and once for the addition of a similar amount to the before-tax margin. Consequently, with a marginal tax rate of 50 percent, the additional tax paid by operating interests per barrel of net working interest is equal to the previous net depletion deduction.[149] Moreover, since after-tax margins are in the long run restored, there is no presumed adverse dividend effect in the long run. It appears, therefore, that operating interests would pay *net* to the Treasury additional taxes per barrel of net working interest production equal in amount to the net depletion deduction—*not* some fraction of it representing the marginal tax rate, with that reduced further by an adverse dividend effect.

Total Effect on Industry Taxes

The *total* effect on tax payments of the industry (including royalty owners) would depend on the way in which the industry restored after-tax margins. Assume that unit costs remain constant, profit margins being restored by increasing prices by the full amount of the previous net depletion deduction. For operating interests, the increase in taxes would be as described above. For royalty owners (whose share has also been increased in price, of course), the addi-

[149] See the example on p. 106 presented in connection with the discussion of price effects of eliminating percentage depletion.

tional taxes paid would be equal to their average effective marginal tax rate multiplied by the sum of their original net depletion deduction and the increase in price. Under the assumptions made in the estimate of impact revenue effects above,[150] their taxes per barrel of royalty interest would increase by 60 percent of the previous net depletion deduction (30 percent $\times$ 2 $\times$ net depletion deduction). If total production were unaffected, then, the total revenue effect would be twice that indicated above, or $1,738 million a year. There would, however, be some decrease in total production due to the price elasticity effect. Assume a 20 percent price increase (based on an assumed net depletion deduction of 20 percent of gross income) and a price elasticity of demand of .30. Production would be reduced by 6 percent (20 percent $\times$ .30), and the increase in tax payments by the industry would be only 94 percent of $1,738 million a year, or $1,634 million a year.

Now assume, in contrast, that following elimination of percentage depletion, profit margins after taxes would be restored wholly by reducing costs, prices remaining constant. Taxes paid by operating interests per barrel of net working interest would increase in the same amount as previously indicated, and there would be no adverse effect from the price elasticity of demand. The total effect on taxes paid would depend on the kind of cost reduction effected. If costs were reduced simply by using capacity more intensively, royalty owners' tax liabilities per barrel of production would be increased by an amount equal to their marginal tax rate multiplied by their previous net depletion deduction. The total increase in tax liability thus would be somewhat less than in the case of a price increase to restore profit margins. If lease bonuses and royalties were reduced as a means of restoring profit margins, the tax liabilities of royalty owners would remain approximately the same as before the elimination of percentage depletion—exactly the same if the previous net depletion deduction is assumed to be the same for both royalty owners and operating interests. If profit margins were restored by reducing the number of wells drilled and equipped to produce a given amount of oil, then the increased tax liability of operating interests and royalty owners would be offset to some degree by the decreased tax liabilities of all those companies (and

[150] P. 112.

their stockholders) engaged in selling goods and services used in well drilling and maintenance. It would be impossible to estimate this effect with any degree of accuracy.

Longer-run Effects

The discussion thus far suggests that elimination of percentage depletion for oil and gas production might in the long run—after full adjustment to the elimination—result in increases in federal income tax revenues by amounts as high as $1.6 billion a year and as low as, say, $1.2 billion a year, on the basis of current production rates and prices. However, the discussion has ignored one rather significant effect that would tend to reduce long-run revenue gains as well as several relatively remote and incidental effects that might reduce long-run revenue gains of all governments combined.

1. The first of these was introduced in an earlier section. It is the effect of owners of interests in oil and gas properties avoiding income tax liability at ordinary rates by converting future income to capital gains. In doing so they also establish a cost basis for the purchaser that is an effective substitute for percentage depletion as a tax saver (but not as an income generator, of course). In the light of the earlier discussion of the capital gains device as applied in the oil and gas industry, it is enough here to say that the estimated revenue gains cited above are entirely too high to be realistic—unless, of course, the capital gains feature in our income tax laws were appropriately modified concurrently with the elimination of percentage depletion. A realistic analysis must take account of the possibilities of tax avoidance that the capital gains feature offers to many owners of oil and gas interests.

If percentage depletion were eliminated, the principal beneficiaries of the capital gains alternative would be royalty owners and owners of relatively small companies or individual operating interests. Few large companies could hope to find buyers on satisfactory terms. Although it is to be expected that use of the capital gains device would be most intense during the early, painful period of adjustment, it seems entirely possible that there would be substantial long-run effects on the structure and procedures of the industry. For example, the capital gains device might remain sufficiently attractive after the early stages of adjustment to warrant the setting up of specialized exploration and development firms that would sell discovered and developed properties to large integrated companies; and the latter might gradually withdraw from this phase of the industry. If so, the long-run tax revenue benefits of eliminating percentage depletion might be small indeed. It is possible, of course, that the Internal Revenue Service or the Congress would take steps to preclude use of the capital gains device in the ordinary course of business, but for individual royalty owners and producers—including "outsiders"—the device would be a readily available means of avoiding tax liabilities. Just how much this effect would reduce the Treasury's total revenue gains is, of course, completely impossible to say.[151]

2. The "remote and incidental effects" of eliminating percentage depletion that might limit long-run revenue gains of all governments combined are associated with the manner of restoring after-tax profit margins of producers. If the increased income tax burden were fully shifted forward in the form of price increases, there would be a small adverse price elasticity effect upon the consumption of petroleum and its products—small because the *relative* prices of oil and gas would not be affected as much as their absolute prices, and the (relative) price elasticity of demand for oil and gas is undoubtedly very low.[152] Nonetheless, there would be *some* adverse effect. With regard to taxes based on physical units of production or consumption—e.g., some state severance taxes and state and federal gasoline taxes—there would be a corresponding adverse effect on revenues. Some idea of the possible magnitude of this revenue reduction is given by the fact that in 1960 total state and federal severance and excise taxes on oil and gas and

---

[151] It is worth noting incidentally that while use of the capital gains device would save taxes for the taxpayer in the long run, it would accelerate payments to the Treasury. The increase in Treasury revenues thus might be very large in the first year or two of adjustment to the elimination of percentage depletion. Moreover, discouragement of new exploration and development in consequence of the elimination of percentage depletion would result in reduced current deductions for dry holes, other unsuccessful exploration expense, and intangible drilling costs, thus tending to increase current tax revenues from a given volume of production.

[152] See notes 138 and 139.

petroleum products amounted to $5.7 billion.[153] A reduction of consumption by as much as 5 percent would decrease such revenues by nearly $0.3 billion.[154] On the other hand, with regard to taxes based on the *value* of production or consumption—e.g., some state severance taxes—oil and gas price increases would result in increased revenues, since the price elasticity of demand is undoubtedly less than unity.

If the increased tax burden resulting from elimination of percentage depletion were absorbed through cost reductions—that is, without any increase in prices—there would be neither gains nor losses of revenues from such taxes as severance and gasoline taxes. Leaving aside the matter of still more remote effects, therefore, total revenue gains of all governments combined would be larger if operators adjusted to elimination of percentage depletion by reducing costs than if they adjusted by raising prices. This would be true particularly if the cost reductions mean that labor and capital are freed and find employment elsewhere, thus adding to the nation's product.

Whether oil and gas operators' adjustments to elimination of percentage depletion took the form of cost reductions or price increases, there would result in the economy as a whole some change in relative prices, the structure of input-output relations, and the distribution of income by size and function. Such changes could hardly fail to affect total tax receipts of federal, state, and local governments, but it is impossible to judge the probable direction and magnitude of the revenue effect.

Conclusion

In conclusion, the tax revenue effects of eliminating percentage depletion are highly uncertain. Total federal, state, and local

[153] Mid-Continent Oil and Gas Association, *op. cit.*, p. 90, citing Tax Foundation, Inc., *Facts and Figures on Government Finance, 1959–1960*, Tables 89, 128, and 129.

[154] If the relative prices of relevant products should rise by 10 percent, price elasticity of demand would have to be .50 to result in a 5 percent reduction in consumption. In the author's opinion, the price elasticity of demand for oil and gas (or products) is not that high, and a 10 percent rise in *relative* prices in consequence of elimination of percentage depletion would be most unlikely.

revenues taken together would probably be increased, but the gain might well be as modest as a few hundred million dollars a year, and the federal government might make gains partly at the expense of state and local governments. Under the most favorable circumstances—adjustment to the change through cost reductions of operators, re-employment of freed resources elsewhere in the economy, and restriction of use of the capital gains device to avoid increased income tax liability—total revenue gains might be in the range of $1.5 billion to $2.0 billion a year. Due to the probably very low price elasticity of demand for oil and gas, it seems most unlikely that even under the most unfavorable circumstances there would result a reduction in total tax revenues from elimination of percentage depletion.

CHAPTER X

Summary of Conference Discussion

THE CONFERENCE DISCUSSION covered the following topics: (1) risk and tax neutrality, (2) national defense, (3) conservation, (4) the relative price effects of eliminating or reducing the degree of distinctive tax treatment, and (5) the effects of adopting various alternative schemes of differential tax treatment. The first four of these headings correspond to issues analyzed in the background paper; the fifth topic was not analyzed in the background paper. Three issues examined in the background paper—oil and gas as "wasting assets," capital gains treatment of the sale of oil and gas properties, and the consequences for tax revenues of changing the rate of percentage depletion—were discussed during the conference only incidentally in connection with other subjects. For purposes of achieving greater coherence in the summary, there is some chronological rearrangement of the discussion, but each portion of the discussion appears under its appropriate subject heading.

In keeping with the spirit of free discussion sought at the conference, the arguments and points of view expressed are recorded here with no identification of their authors. The names of three participants are mentioned in the summary, but not to identify direct contributions to the conference discussion. They are mentioned solely to identify particular analytical approaches, associated with their names in the professional literature, that were discussed at length in the conference. Without such identification, much of the summary would be unintelligible to the nonparticipant reader.

It should be emphasized that the following is a condensed record of discussion and not a compilation of conclusions agreed upon by the conferees. No poll of the conferees was taken on any argument, proposal, or point of view offered in the discussion. Beyond that, the participants were so numerous and the discussion moved so freely and rapidly from one point to another that no accurate impression could have been formed as to the extent of agreement on most of the matters discussed. The presence in the record of an unchallenged statement should not be taken to imply general acceptance of it. Similarly, evidence of vigorous counter-argument need not suggest general dissent.

Risk and Tax Neutrality

In the background paper, risk was regarded as a real cost affecting relative prices and the allocation of resources among industries. It was argued that if risk differs among industries, income taxation at uniform nominal rates is not neutral in its effect on resource allocation. Resources tend to be repelled from the relatively high risk industries and attracted to the relatively low risk industries. The effect of differential risk, the argument continued, depends on differential capital intensity: given the degree of risk, resources tend to be repelled from the more capital intensive industries and attracted to the less capital intensive industries. It was further argued, then, that if the oil and gas industry is markedly more risky and capital intensive than manufacturing as a whole, the distinctive tax treatment of income from oil and gas production may be consistent with tax neutrality as between these two industry groups. This conclusion is in sharp contrast with that of other studies of this question, principally those of Arnold C. Harberger and Peter O. Steiner,[155] who use an analytical model substantially different from that employed in the background paper.

The Harberger-Steiner model is constructed in terms of dis-

[155] See pp. 49–52 above for a description of the subject studies and references to original literature.

counted cash flows.[156] It indicates the allocative effects of distinctive tax treatment by showing whether such treatment renders unequal the present values of equivalent streams of income. In using this model, Harberger and Steiner abstract from differences in risk among industries and make no specific assumption about tax incidence. It was noted in the background paper that the model readily accommodates an assumption of differential risk (in the effective rate of discount); but in the belief that it could not accommodate assumptions of tax shifting and differential capital intensity, the author of the background paper devised another model. The latter (hereinafter called the McDonald model) indicates the allocative effects of distinctive tax treatment by comparing equilibrium relative prices in a no-tax situation with equilibrium relative prices in a specified tax situation. It asks the question: Given differences in risk and capital intensity among industries, how would relative product prices be affected by the introduction of a proportional corporation income tax? Change in relative prices as a result of the specified tax is taken to indicate that the tax would not be neutral in its effect. In using this model, McDonald assumed full tax shifting in the sense that after-tax rates of return on capital remain constant; he further assumed that capital intensities remain constant.

The Harberger-Steiner analysis led to the conclusion that the present degree of differential tax treatment of income from oil and gas production definitely is not neutral, inducing an excessive application of resources to that industry. The McDonald analysis, in contrast, indicated that the present degree of differential tax treatment may be consistent with allocative neutrality. Much of the discussion in the opening session of the conference was devoted to these analyses, the general assumptions made in each, and the inferences derived from each on the specific assumption of differential risk and capital intensity among industries.

There was wide agreement among the conferees that the degree of risk and capital intensity are important in evaluating the distinctive tax treatment of income from oil and gas production. In the absence of special risks or unusual capital requirements, most participants seemed to agree, relatively more capital would be

---

[156] See Appendix B for the algebra of the discounted cash flow model.

attracted to the industry than if there were no income tax. They held that differential taxation would lead to this result, rather than a mere increase in relative profits, because they believe that entry is free enough to assure that in the long run profits would be driven down to the competitive level. The consequence would be a misallocation of resources unless there were an overriding national interest in stimulating investment in the industry.

It was also widely agreed that any special risks or capital requirements are real costs. The position taken in the background paper, and supported by some conference participants, was that the oil and gas industry may be especially risky and capital intensive and, if so, that application of the same tax rate to that industry as to all other industries would result in an inefficient allocation of resources. The participants who supported this position held that some degree of differential taxation might be necessary for efficient resource allocation, but they did not contend that exactly the present degree of tax differentiation could be justified on these grounds alone.

Other participants argued that, even granted the assumption of special risk and high capital intensity, the distinctive tax provisions applying to the oil and gas industry could not be justified on grounds of allocative efficiency. Arguments given, but not necessarily accepted by all of those who took this position, were that: (1) the existing tax provisions go much further than would be necessary to compensate for any plausible degree of differential risk, (2) loss offsets greatly reduce the adverse influence of income taxation on risky investment, and (3) especially high capital intensity can cause misallocation only if it is assumed that the corporation income tax is shifted forward.

Some participants challenged the assumption that profits in the oil industry are held to the competitive level because of free entry. They feel that a condition of administered prices and limited entry might exist in the industry and that differential taxation may result in unnecessarily high profits rather than excessive capital investment.

Empirical questions relating to the degree of risk in the industry were discussed, including (1) the composition and adequacy of McDonald's sample data, (2) the significance of book rates of return, (3) the industry's investment criteria in the exploration-production and other phases, and (4) the significance of dry-hole ratios.

It was noted that an exchange in the professional literature over the McDonald model and its application had established that the sample from which McDonald derived his data was dominated by firms engaged largely in foreign production and thus was not necessarily representative of either the domestic industry or the industry as a whole. Removal from the sample of firms with foreign production (which would not leave a representative sample even of the domestic industry) reduces the indicated "neutral" special exemption for oil and gas production from 22 percent to 14 percent of gross income, the former figure being an approximation of the actual effective special exemption.[157]

The rate of return estimates used in the background paper are book rates of return. The objection was made that book rates of return are inappropriate indicators of the rates of return investors expect and get on a cash-flow basis. The former may deviate substantially from the latter, the relevant rates of return, because the two do not equally reflect variations in the time distribution of investments and cash flows. Some support of efforts to measure typical rates of return from accounting statements was voiced, however, if only because cash-flow rates of return are inaccessible. Several participants objected to using observed rates of return as indicators of risk on the grounds that rate-of-return differentials may reflect market imperfections and distinctive tax provisions.

Some discussion centered on the question whether a higher rate of return (signifying greater riskiness) is demanded in the exploratory-production phase of the oil and gas industry than in other phases of the industry. In reply to questions, several participants who are familiar with investment criteria in the industry said that it is. At least one exception to the rule was noted, however; and referring to another company of which he has knowledge, one participant indicated that the ratio of the relevant rates of return (based on

[157] See Douglas H. Eldridge, "Rate of Return, Resource Allocation and Percentage Depletion," *National Tax Journal*, Vol. 15 (June 1962), pp. 215–16; and Stephen L. McDonald, "Percentage Depletion and Tax Neutrality: A Reply to Messrs. Musgrave and Eldridge," *National Tax Journal*, Vol. 15 (September 1962) pp. 324–25, for further details.

discounted cash flow) is less than the two-to-one ratio used in the background paper to estimate a "neutral" special exemption for the oil and gas industry.

There was a lengthy discussion of the question whether the nearly constant annual industry-wide exploratory dry-hole ratios[158] are consistent with the allegation of great risk or great uncertainty in the industry. (The classical distinction made by Frank H. Knight between risk and uncertainty was recognized, some participants believing the difference in practice to be one of degree. According to that distinction, risk pertains to situations in which there is a known probability distribution of possible returns on investment, while uncertainty pertains to situations in which the probability distribution of possible returns on investment is unknown or unknowable.) It was suggested that the nearly constant dry hole ratios are inconsistent with great uncertainty, since they indicate definite probabilities for the industry as a whole, but are consistent with almost any degree of risk for the individual firm, depending upon the scale of drilling activity. This view was contested by some participants, who argued that "uncertainty" properly describes the situation faced by individual firms and the industry at large in areas never before explored. Furthermore, dry hole ratios are inadequate evidence of the chances of economic success in exploratory drilling, it was argued, since exploratory ventures differ greatly in cost and, if successful, result in discoveries of widely varying value. It was pointed out that if success in exploration is measured in terms of discoveries per well or per foot drilled, the industry success ratio varies greatly from year to year. One large company's experience was cited to the effect that the value of discoveries per dollar of exploratory inputs has varied from as little as ten cents to as much as three dollars between five-year periods.

National Defense

In discussing its relation to distinctive tax treatment of income from oil and gas production, the background paper defined national defense as preparation for either nuclear or limited war. The distinctive tax provisions were discussed in the paper in terms of their

[158] See pp. 36 and 40 above.

possible contribution to (1) divertible oil and gas capacity (capacity used to satisfy civilian demand during peacetime but divertible to war-related uses as needed) or to (2) reserve oil and gas capacity (capacity withheld from civilian uses in peacetime to assure availability for war-related uses as needed or to replace imported oil in any use). There was widespread feeling among the conferees that the statement of the national defense problem in terms of preparation for actual war is too limited and thus does not adequately pose the issue of the possible contribution of distinctive tax treatment to national defense.

It was pointed out that oil and gas capacity in the control of the United States is one of the country's instruments in the cold war. In addition, the Suez crisis was cited as an example of a kind of emergency short of war in which the ability quickly to expand petroleum production in the Western Hemisphere could be both an immediate economic stabilizer for the United States and its allies and a deterrent to potential aggressors. It was argued that the very size of the domestic industry, especially as it affects the fraction of consumption supplied from vulnerable foreign sources, is a factor in this nation's ability to achieve its foreign policy aims without direct resort to military action. One discussant, granting all this, nonetheless took the position that defense needs could be described in terms of either divertible or reserve capacity to produce, transport, and process oil and gas.

There was some effort in the discussion to specify the content of an adequate defense policy with respect to oil and gas. One participant suggested an approach in terms of building up the nation's strength in general rather than concentrating on capacity in critical materials. Under this approach one would consider such questions as the elimination of bottlenecks and the provision of a transportation system whose particular modes and routes could meet needs in any kind of possible international emergency. Others suggested the desirability of dispersing petroleum producing capacity, of encouraging the development of capacity in the less vulnerable areas of the world, and of assuring spare capacity not only in the producing phase of the industry but in transportation and refining facilities as well. The point was made that control of foreign production by United States interests, by denying control to potential enemies, may strengthen the nation's defense position.

Having brought out the complexity of defining an adequate defense policy with respect to oil and gas, the discussion moved on to the question of the possible contribution of distinctive tax treatment to identifiable objectives. The opinion seemed widely held among the group that differential taxation *per se* does not assure *reserve* capacity as defined above. In this view, persistent reserve capacity is associated with the systems of regulating production in several of the major producing states; reserve capacity from this source would arise with or without distinctive tax treatment, the amount of such capacity depending in part upon the degree of distinctive tax treatment. Moreover, many of the discussants believe that reserve producing capacity arising from state production regulation does not assure similar reserve capacity in transportation and refining facilities. The provision of *divertible*, or simply enlarged, producing capacity is another matter. There seemed to be little doubt among the group that the total output of the oil and gas industry, including both foreign and domestic production, is larger than it would have been without distinctive tax treatment. (Some uncertainty was expressed, however, in view of the possibility that production regulation and administered pricing may divert the incentive effects of differential effective tax rates into inefficiencies and higher profits.) Some participants contended strongly that the enlarged output of the industry is a definite contribution to national defense because the enlargement represents greater existing capacity, in transportation and refining as well as in minerals production proper, that may be diverted from civilian to war-related uses in an emergency.

Considerable discussion centered on the question whether the distinctive tax provisions applying to income of United States producers both at home and abroad have any effect on the relative size of the domestic industry. Some participants argued that the provisions are more favorable to domestic production because, in contrast with the situation abroad, there are numerous near-marginal independent explorer-producers at home whose survival depends on the existing tax arrangements. Also expressed was the opposing view that since special tax benefits represent a larger fraction of the gross income of foreign producers than of domestic producers, elimination of the benefits would be relatively helpful to the domestic industry. Some discussants felt that the distinctive tax provisions have no significant effect on the division of production as between foreign and domestic sources, but that to eliminate the provisions only as applied to foreign production would surely be relatively stimulating to the domestic industry. It was noted incidentally that elimination of distinctive tax treatment of income from foreign production would not necessarily increase United States Treasury revenues, since the domestic foreign tax credit encourages foreign treasuries to absorb at least as much as the United States tax liability.

Even if one concedes national defense benefits from distinctive tax provisions in the oil and gas industry, there remains the question of the relation of these benefits to their cost. It was argued by several conferees that the costs might well outweigh the benefits. They pointed out that to encourage through differential taxation enlarged output or reserve capacity in the oil and gas industry implies reduced output or more limited capacity in other industries, given full employment as a normal condition. The result may be a less efficient allocation of resources and discouragment of industries of equal or greater essentiality to national defense than oil and gas production. Some participants took the position, in reply, that no other industries are more essential to national defense than oil and gas and some are less; that, therefore, a diversion of resources from other pursuits in general to the production of oil and gas must be a positive contribution to national security. Since full employment is not the obviously normal condition in the economy, one discussant observed, greater output of oil and gas is not necessarily bought at the cost of other products. A somewhat different kind of cost of using differential taxation to secure greater current output of oil and gas was noted by one participant, who pointed out that more current output might mean less future output if new reserves are to be found only under conditions of increasing costs. He suggested that long-run national defense interests might best be served by discouraging current consumption and deferring exploitation of domestic reserves.

Another way of appraising the cost of using differential taxation to achieve national defense objectives is to consider other ways of doing it. One suggestion was to eliminate distinctive tax treatment and rely on the import quota system to assure an appropriate domestic capacity. To this the objection was raised that so long as the size and basis of import quotas are uncertain, the desired incentive to domestic exploration would not be provided. A second suggestion was to encourage the development of substitutes for oil and gas. In this connection it was noted that the domestic price of crude petroleum is now not far below the level at which shale oil might become competitive. In reply to the proposition that stockpiling petroleum in the form of developed reserves in natural reservoirs would be a more certain means of securing a given amount of emergency capacity, it was argued that our experience with stockpiling other critical materials indicates that the method is expensive and perhaps conducive to irregularities.

One discussant expressed his doubt that if the Congress had set out to achieve a given national defense objective it would have settled on distinctive tax treatment as the appropriate way to do it. In response, the observation was made that national defense was in fact one of the considerations in the earliest provision of distinctive tax treatment for the oil and gas industry, but that the case for differential taxation had never rested wholly on the national defense argument.

Conservation

Relatively little time was devoted to a discussion of conservation in relation to differential taxation, partly because there seemed to be fewer areas of disagreement on this subject than on others considered.

In the background paper conservation was defined as the optimum time distribution of resource exploitation. It was argued that solution of the time distribution problem in the case of a "stock" resource involves the same data and procedures as any capital use problem. One discussant suggested as an alternative definition of conservation, which several others also preferred, governmental *alteration* of the time distribution of resource exploitation to correct an "unwise" rate of current use. Presumably such government action is taken when it is believed that ordinary market forces would not induce a time distribution of exploitation consistent with the public interest. (For instance, the government might intervene to slow down the rate of exploitation of given resources because private shortsightedness or imperfections in the capital markets would lead to exploitation that is excessively rapid from the social point of view.)

In the ensuing discussion it was pointed out that on the same sort of premise about the adequacy of market forces the two definitions of conservation would lead to the same sort of action. It was noted that under either definition conservation could require acceleration, no change, or deceleration of the rate of exploitation, depending on circumstances. The discussion also indicated virtually general agreement in the group that the conservation problem cannot be formulated in purely physical terms.

The suggestion was made by one conferee that percentage depletion *per se* (as distinct from the special expensing provisions) has no bearing on conservation apart from the allocative effects previously discussed in the conference. But it was pointed out that, insofar as percentage depletion lowers the current price of oil and gas, it affects the time rate of exploitation of oil and gas resources. On the premise that conservation demands a slowing down of oil and gas consumption in the present, one participant observed, percentage depletion would seem to be contrary to the interests of conservation. Another commented that whether accelerated use is to be regarded as desirable or undesirable depends on the assumption made as to the supply of undiscovered resources.

Special expensing provisions affect oil and gas conservation, according to some of the discussants, chiefly by encouraging unnecessary drilling of wells. As explained in the background paper (pp. 25–26), expensing capital outlays as they occur rather than amortizing them over the productive life of assets acquired reduces the effective cost of the assets. This results from the well-known principle that early tax savings through deductions for capital recovery are worth more than later ones at any positive rate of discount. Effectively lower-cost wells, in turn, encourage the drilling of more wells to acquire a given amount of productive capacity. However, several participants felt that the overdrilling problem results almost entirely from the system of state regulation and is only marginally affected by the fact that the expensing provision reduces the net cost of well drilling.

Price Effects

At the outset it was evident that the background paper's analysis of the relative price effects of eliminating or reducing differential taxation of the oil and gas industry needed to be clarified. Most of the analysis in the paper is based on the assumption (consistent with reality at the time of writing) of excess capacity and substantial wastes arising from regulatory procedures in the industry. The conclusion was reached that, following an increase in the effective tax rate on oil and gas income, prices of oil and gas might remain unchanged or rise by any amount up to 20 percent, depending partly on induced regulatory changes, and the reader was left without a clear rule as to the general effect. The clarification offered to the discussants was as follows:

If at the time of the hypothesized increase in the effective tax rate the industry was in equilibrium and operating at the optimum rate of utilization of capacity, with no wasteful investment reflected in that capacity, the adjustment to higher taxes would surely lead to higher prices in the eventual new equilibrium. The price increase would be less than the tax increase per unit of product, however, due to some upward slope in its long-run supply curve. An upward sloping long-run supply curve signifies that the firms making up the industry (and those that might be added to it through new entry) have different unit costs, due to long-lasting qualitative differences (e.g., in management or producing properties). The long-run cost of the product at the margin corresponds to the long-run unit cost of the highest-cost firm that can earn enough net income to justify its remaining in the industry. (Lower-cost firms are said to enjoy "rents," i.e., net incomes in excess of the amounts necessary to justify their remaining in the industry.) Now if the costs of all firms in the industry were increased by raising the effective rate of income taxation, given the demand for the product, previously marginal firms would be eliminated, and some (lower-cost) previously supramarginal firms would become marginal. Accordingly, the *net* effect on product cost at the margin would be the result of the *increase* in tax paid per unit and the *decrease* in cost at the margin through the elimination of previously marginal firms.

With initial excess capacity and wasteful investment reflected in that capacity as a result of regulatory procedures, on the other hand, the adjustment to higher tax rates would not necessarily lead to higher prices in an eventual new equilibrium at optimum capacity utilization. As in the earlier case, reductions of rents might help to hold down prices. In addition, the reduction of excess capacity (through a reduced rate of investment and the elimination of marginal firms) would in time lower unit costs, and the initial distress of the industry might induce cost-reducing improvements in regulatory practices (e.g., wider spacing of wells). However, to the extent that the initial excess capacity would have led to lower prices independently of the assumed tax change, the effect of the latter would be to raise prices over what they would have been without any tax change. The general rule, accordingly, is that eliminating or reducing the degree of distinctive tax treatment of income from oil and gas production would, in some degree, raise the relative prices of oil and gas.

Some discussion in the conference was devoted to further refining the above statement. Several participants were concerned with the implication that the burden of increased oil and gas taxes would fall solely on consumers of oil and gas. It was pointed out that in the period of transition to a new equilibrium the burden would be borne (in decreasing degree with time) by capital. Only in the new equilibrium would the net increase in cost be borne by oil and gas consumers. Moreover, if total tax revenues remained constant, implying reduced taxes elsewhere in the economy, consumers of other products would benefit; and, if the elimination or reduction of differentially low taxation of oil and gas income improved the allocation of resources (explicitly not conceded by several conferees), consumers as a whole would benefit from the change. An improved allocation of resources would mean that in new uses the affected resources would produce more at the margin than in previous uses. Hence there would be a larger total product from the same quantity of resources.

The influence of rents (defined above), reflected in the slope of the industry's long-run supply curve, also was further clarified. It was noted that rents arise not only from the technical superiority of some firms, but also from landowners' possession of deposits capable of returning more than enough to cover costs of development and recovery and the differential marginal tax rates that may obtain under the United States corporate and personal income tax systems. One discussant suggested that possibly induced changes in imports might further qualify the price-increasing effect of taxing oil and gas income more heavily. If the world price of oil should be substantially unaffected by a change in United States tax laws, and if imports into the United States were free, the domestic price of oil would similarly be substantially unaffected. A firm and unchanged system of import quotas, on the other hand, would allow the domestic price of oil to rise with increased taxes. As for the price of gas, it was noted that public regulation might restrain any proposed increases. Since oil and gas are to a significant degree joint products, oil prices might have to bear all of the burden of adjustment to increased taxes; and those prices, therefore, might rise more than the increase in taxes paid per unit of product.

In the background paper (pp. 105–06) it was estimated that the upper limit of the price increase resulting from the elimination of percentage depletion *per se*, the expensing provisions remaining unchanged, would be the increase in taxes paid per unit, or 20 percent of the prechange price. The effect of the conference discussion was to suggest that, taking oil and gas together and abstracting from individual petroleum products, the actual price increase would be significantly less; but lack of knowledge about all the relevant variables precluded any precise estimate of how much less.

The role of state regulatory commissions in the price-making process was discussed at some length. The background paper had stated that the system of production regulation geared to quantity demanded at the going price, which system prevails in several of the more important producing states, would be an aid in adjusting prices upward following an effective tax increase in the industry. Some conferees interpreted the regulatory system as a price-fixing device, or at least the equivalent of a "ratchet" mechanism which allows prices to rise but not to fall. Others contended that the system has no specific price objectives but is designed to allocate the quantity demanded, at whatever price prevails, among producers in the jurisdiction in such a way as to assure capacity output from legislatively-defined marginal wells and proportionate sharing of the remaining market by supramarginal wells. It was argued that within the limits imposed by these restraints, which are not imposed by all major producing states, prices are free to rise and fall in response to changes in cost and demand. Under either interpretation of the role of production regulation, in any case, the system would be a help rather than a hindrance to upward price adjustments following effective tax increases.

The price elasticity of demand for oil and gas also was the subject of some discussion. A number of the participants feel that the demand for both of these minerals is quite price-inelastic, well below unity. Their opinion is based largely on the proposition that in many major uses there are no close substitutes for natural gas and the products of petroleum, especially gasoline, and that there is no close substitute for petroleum as a source of gasoline. It was conceded that the elasticity of demand for such products as heating and boiler oils and for boiler-firing natural gas may be quite high. Some conferees went further, arguing that even the demand for gasoline is substantially price-elastic. The growing use of compact cars, partly for reasons of fuel economy, was cited as a source of such elasticity, especially in the long run. It was further pointed out that if petroleum prices were even slightly above present levels, shale oil might offer a close substitute source of gasoline.

One participant said that if the price-elasticity of demand for oil and gas is quite low (and he is of the opinion that it is), then the misallocative effect, if any, of the differential taxation of oil and gas income is correspondingly low. A low price-elasticity of demand means that a given percentage decrease in the relative price of the product would be associated with a smaller percentage increase in the quantity of the product demanded. Accordingly, the percentage increase in the quantity of resources used in producing the product also would be relatively low. He went on to argue that the presumably lowered prices of oil and gas due to differential taxation provide an offset to any misallocation effect: consumers of oil and gas have more income to save or to spend on other products. To this the reply was made that the offset is illusory, since the lower prices of oil and gas achieved through tax policy must be paid for in the form of higher prices on other products or in the form of higher personal taxes to provide a direct subsidy to oil and gas production. Moreover, if there is misallocation, then consumers as a whole are worse off, because total available resources yield a smaller total product.

Alternative Methods of Tax Treatment

At the final session of the conference the following five methods of differential tax treatment of income from oil and gas production alternative to the present methods were offered for discussion:

1. Keep percentage depletion as is, but require the capitalization of intangible development costs and make them recoverable through cost or percentage depletion.
2. Eliminate all provisions for depletion and depreciation, and allow the immediate expensing of all capital outlays as made.
3. Same as #2, but with capital gains treatment allowed on proceeds from sale of oil and gas properties only to the extent that gross proceeds exceed accumulated expenses on all properties.
4. Same as #2, but with no capital gains treatment allowed on sales of mineral properties.
5. Keep the existing percentage depletion and expensing provisions, but add a limitation on the total allowable accumulated amount of percentage plus cost depletion.

Some participants observed that the list includes neither the retention of the present tax treatment unmodified nor complete elimination of distinctive tax treatment of oil and gas income. Note was also taken of the fact that the above list by no means exhausts possible alternatives in the range between no change and complete elimination of distinctive treatment. Other alternatives specifically mentioned included differentiation between domestic and foreign producers, or between explorer-producers and other producers, or between large and small operators; and the elimination of all special deductions and expensing provisions, but with the Treasury sharing in losses as it shares in profits at the going tax rate. A number of participants objected to discussion of the listed alternatives on the ground that they had not been previously presented to the conferees for study and had not been discussed in the background paper. The understanding reached was that the purpose of discussing the above alternatives was to clarify the effects of the various existing special tax features by considering the consequences of their elimination or modification, one by one; and that the fact of discussion need not imply that the conferees, individually or as a group, agree that there should be some, but a lesser degree of, differential tax treatment of income from oil and gas.

ALTERNATIVE 1. In the discussion it was pointed out that the indicated change in the treatment of intangible development costs would not merely eliminate the cost-reducing effects of immediate tax deduction (explained above, p. 129); it would altogether preclude separate and additional deduction of intangible costs where percentage depletion was used. Several reasons were offered in the discussion for believing that Alternative 1 would have somewhat different effects than equivalent tax increases through reduction of percentage depletion. One participant expressed the opinion that the intangible expensing provision is more valuable to the smaller operators, who drill a number of wells disproportionate to their assets or production, while percentage depletion is more valuable to the larger companies with extensive highly productive, economically developed properties offering maximum opportunity to raise the effective percentage depletion rate through aggregation. The expensing provision is more favorable to development drilling than to exploration and production *per se*, another discussant observed, while percentage depletion rewards the passive producer as well as holding out an incentive to exploration and development. Another difference noted is that expensed exploration outlays, and expensed development outlays, when they exceed the income from the property on which they are made, are deductible from any income of the taxpayer. Percentage depletion, on the other hand, is deductible only from the income of the property producing it. Elimination of the expensing provision might be particularly discouraging, therefore, to operators with income from sources other than properties on which percentage depletion could be taken.

ALTERNATIVE 2. This choice, the discussion brought out, would invite operators to write off capital outlays against available income, realizing tax savings at the effective income tax rate, and then to sell out for capital gains and incur a maximum tax liability of 25 percent. Particular objection was expressed to creating a situation in which tax losses become assets in merger arrangements, thus favoring concentration of production. It was pointed out also that this alternative would encourage excessive drilling; the present limitation of percentage depletion to 50 percent of net income, property by property, now tends to discourage excessive drilling.

ALTERNATIVE 3. Much the same observations were made about this alternative as about Alternative 2, although it was noted that Alternative 3 would be less beneficial to those with "outside" income against which to write off capital outlays. Speaking of the whole capital gains problem, both in the oil and gas industry and in other sectors of the economy, one discussant said that the Internal Revenue Service has been unduly lenient in allowing capital gains treatment of proceeds that really represent ordinary income converted to present value. The reply was that court decisions have severely limited the discretion of the Service.

ALTERNATIVE 4. The objection was raised to this choice that it would be inequitable and politically unfeasible to disallow capital gains treatment of proceeds from the sale of oil and gas properties while allowing it in other cases. Capital gains treatment of oil and gas property sales was defended as a kind of incentive to compensate for the fact that many of the losses in the search for oil and gas are incurred by explorers who never have sufficient success to cover all their costs. If against the known chances of substantial losses potential explorers can weigh the prospect of especially favorable tax treatment of any discoveries that may be made, whether they are operated by the finders or sold, more persons and companies with modest resources are encouraged to assume the risks of exploration, it was argued.

ALTERNATIVE 5. It was argued in the case of this alternative that if the limitation on accumulated allowable percentage depletion were expressed in terms of actual capital outlays, it would under certain conditions encourage wasteful capital outlays. Thus, if the outlays themselves were tax deductible, as is now the case with most types of outlays, and if allowable percentage depletion were enlarged by the same amount as the outlays, then at a tax rate in excess of 50 percent the undiscounted sum of the tax savings would exceed the cost of any outlays made. Similar results would follow from a tax rate in excess of 50 percent if the outlays themselves were not deductible but allowable percentage depletion were set at two or more times actual outlays.

This point was qualified somewhat in the ensuing discussion, in which it was noted that current rules might preclude the use of wasteful expenditures to enlarge allowable depletion. One of these is the limitation of allowable depletion to 50 percent of net income, property by property. In addition, the rule that allowable depletion must be computed property by property presumably would preclude the use of a wasteful outlay not attributable to a depletable property to increase allowable depletion on that property. It was noted further that capitalized geological and geophysical expenses could not be arbitrarily enlarged after the establishment of production, and that percentage depletion ordinarily would not be used in the case of a purchased property, cost depletion usually providing the larger deduction. One discussant pointed out that Alternative 5 would still leave the capital gains route attractive. After the operator had "used up" his maximum allowable depletion, he could still sell out for capital gains.

Without particular reference to the above five alternatives, the discussion in the final session touched briefly on the question of equity. Several participants expressed the view that present distinctive tax treatment of income from oil and gas production involves significant inequities. Allowing percentage depletion on royalties was offered as an example. The landowner's royalty (if not acquired through purchase) is basically a form of economic rent; that is, it is a form of income not required to call forth a productive activity by its recipient.[159] Yet this form of income is accorded favored treatment in comparison with incomes derived from labor, enterprise, and risk-taking. (One participant observed that since the royalty right is a salable asset, disallowance of percentage depletion would only induce sales for capital gains.) Other instances of inequities noted stem from differences in marginal personal income tax rates: the distinctive tax provisions applying to income from oil

[159] See note 142.

and gas production mean greater tax savings for persons with higher marginal tax rates. It was noted that, aside from the ethical questions, inequities may involve such costs as poorer voluntary compliance with income tax laws. One discussant, agreeing that there are inequities, argued that steps should be taken to eliminate them within the prevailing system of differential taxation. Another said that he could not become concerned about such issues as neutrality so long as great inequities, as he saw them, exist in the tax system.

As the conference drew to a close, several participants commented on the problem posed by the existence of a number of perhaps competing criteria of tax appropriateness, including equity, neutrality, and encouragement of growth, to which each citizen would assign somewhat different relative weights. It was surmised that much of the disagreement in the conference could be traced to the different weights attached to these criteria. But the final note was that, whatever the order of preferences, the problem is one of comparing costs with benefits; and the question remains, in the present approach to the taxation of income from oil and gas production, what is the relation of costs to benefits?

List of Conference Participants

Walter J. Blum
  Professor of Law
  University of Chicago

Harvey E. Brazer
  Professor of Economics
  University of Michigan

Robert D. Calkins
  President
  The Brookings Institution

Mortimer M. Caplin
  Commissioner
  Internal Revenue Service

Lesley Cookenboo
  Manager, Economics Research
    Department
  Richfield Oil Corp. of Calif.

Henry G. Corey
  Director, Economics Division
  Continental Oil Company

Douglas Eldridge
  Professor of Economics
  Claremont Men's College

Charles O. Galvin
  Professor of Law
  Southern Methodist University

Richard Gonzalez
  Director, Finance and Economics
  Humble Oil Company

Richard Goode
  Senior Staff
  The Brookings Institution

Arnold C. Harberger
  Professor of Economics
  University of Chicago

William Henry
  Tax Counsel
  Gulf Oil Company

Robert G. James
  Socony Mobil Oil Company

Minor S. Jameson
  Vice President
  Independent Petroleum Assn.

Richard Kruizenga
  Standard Oil Co. of N.J.

George Koch
  Manager, Tax Department
  Standard Oil Co. of N.J.

Scott C. Lambert
  Standard Oil Company

Warren Law
  Associate Professor of Business
    Administration
  Harvard University

Oscar Lentz
  Associate Professor of Eco-
    nomics
  Colorado School of Mines

Joseph Lerner
  Office of Emergency Planning

Walter J. Levy
  Consultant
  New York City

John H. Lichtblau
  Research Director
  Petroleum Industry Research
    Foundation

Wallace Lovejoy
  Professor of Economics
  Southern Methodist University

James E. Jansen
  Professor of Economics
  Central State College

139

Conference Participants *(Continued)*

Stephen L. McDonald
   Professor of Economics
   University of Texas

James McKie
   Professor of Economics
   Vanderbilt University

Richard A. Musgrave
   Professor of Economics
   Princeton University

Joseph A. Pechman
   Director of Economic Studies
   The Brookings Institution

Sam Schurr
   Director, Energy and Minerals
      Resources Program
   Resources for the Future

Carl S. Shoup
   Professor of Economics
   Columbia University

Dan Throop Smith
   Professor of Finance
   Graduate School of Business Ad-
      ministration
   Harvard University

Peter Steiner
   Professor of Economics
   University of Wisconsin

Stanley S. Surrey
   Assistant Secretary of the
      Treasury

Norman B. Ture
   Director of Tax Studies
   National Bureau of Economic
      Research

Harold Wein
   Chief Economist
   Federal Power Commission

APPENDIX A

Comparative Rates of Return
by Major Industry Division

The First National City Bank of New York has, since 1938, published rates of return on net assets of "leading corporations," grouped by industry divisions. The industry division samples, while not necessarily representative in a strict statistical sense, appear to be large enough to give a reasonably good indication of corporation rates of return in the corresponding divisions of industry in this country. Companies in the petroleum industry sample are divided into two groups: those with integrated operations and those engaged exclusively in finding, developing, and producing oil and gas.[160] In the 1961 sample there were 44 companies with book net assets (as of the first of the year) of $29.4 billion in the former category, and 80 companies with first-of-year book net assets of $1.6 billion in the latter category.

The sample companies, it would appear, account for at least 75 per cent of total domestic petroleum production. Some 26 of the integrated companies in the sample alone accounted for about 60 per cent of total United States production in 1960. The same 26 companies produced about 25 percent more oil abroad than domestically in that year,[161] a

---

[160] Since 1950, the First National City Bank has lumped the two divisions together in its published figures. The author is indebted to Mr. John H. Reedy, Associate Economist of that bank, for supplying the two-division breakdown for the years since 1950.

[161] The percentages in this and the preceding sentence computed by the author on the basis of data supplied by the Economics Department, First National City Bank of New York.

fact which suggests that the rates of return recorded for the "integrated operations" category are strongly influenced by returns on foreign operations. Foreign production appears to be negligible in the "oil and gas production" category. The rates of return recorded for this category reflect domestic operations almost entirely, but the production involved is such a small percentage of total domestic production that these rates of return may not be representative of the entire industry's domestic experience in its finding-developing-producing phase.

Rates of return on net assets of "leading corporations" in the two petroleum industry categories and in manufacturing, mining, and all industry represented in the First National City Bank sample for the years 1938–61 are shown in Table A-1. Here it can be seen that in every year since 1941 the average rate of return of corporations engaged exclusively in oil and gas production (that is, finding, developing, and producing) has been higher than that of integrated companies in the petroleum industry. Similarly, the rate of return in oil and gas production has been higher than that in manufacturing since 1942, higher than that in mining

TABLE A-1. Rate of Return After Taxes on Net Assets of Leading Corporations in Selected Industries, United States, 1938–61 (Percent)

| Year | Petroleum Industry | | Manufacturing | Mining | All Industry |
	Integrated Operations	Oil and Gas Production			
1938	5.0	6.5	4.6	4.2	3.8
1939	5.4	4.8	8.3	4.8	6.3
1940	5.4	4.3	10.5	6.3	7.8
1941	9.9	8.3	12.3	6.8	8.9
1942	7.0	9.0	9.9	7.4	8.5
1943	7.9	10.8	9.6	7.2	8.6
1944	9.7	12.5	9.6	8.0	8.2
1945	8.4	13.2	9.3	7.1	7.7
1946	10.7	12.6	12.1	9.4	9.5
1947	15.8	19.9	17.1	16.0	12.3
1948	22.1	35.9	18.2	20.5	13.6
1949	13.2	21.7	13.9	12.0	11.0
1950	14.9	18.3	17.1	13.2	13.4
1951	16.5	19.5	14.4	13.0	11.4
1952	14.4	16.3	12.3	10.1	10.4
1953	14.3	16.4	12.7	7.9	10.6
1954	13.7	15.3	12.3	8.2	10.3
1955	14.1	16.2	14.9	13.0	11.9
1956	14.6	16.0	13.8	13.8	11.3
1957	13.4	16.5	12.9	9.6	10.6
1958	10.1	11.8	9.8	7.3	8.9
1959	9.9	12.2	11.7	7.8	9.8
1960	10.1	12.5	10.6	8.0	9.1
1961	10.3	12.7	10.1	8.6	8.7

Sources: Petroleum industry divisions: Economics Department, First National City Bank of New York.
All other industry divisions: First National City Bank of New York, Monthly Letter, April issues.

since 1940, and higher than that in all industry taken together since 1941. The lower relative rates of return of the oil and gas production division in the years 1938–42 undoubtedly reflect in large measure the chaotic conditions of the domestic industry during the thirties and its burden of excess capacity extending into the first years of World War II. It is noteworthy in this connection that the rate of return of the oil and gas production division, although lower than in previous years, remained above that of the other industrial divisions in Table A-1 in the years after 1957, despite reduced and virtually static domestic crude oil production, growing excess capacity, and price weakness in the industry. Moreover, it seems significant that the lower rates of return after 1957 have been associated with a decline of about 20 percent in the number of wells drilled in the United States.[162]

Aside from the question of the representativeness of the sample of oil and gas producing firms in the First National City Bank tabulation, one might argue that differences in debt-equity ratios could account for the relationships observed among rates of return on net assets. On an earlier occasion,[163] the present writer analyzed a much larger sample, based on corporation income tax returns, making allowance for differences in debt-equity ratios. The sample used was those corporations reporting net income, filing balance sheets with their income tax returns for the years 1949–51 and 1953–56 inclusive (data for 1952 being unavailable), and classified in Internal Revenue Service compilations as producers of "Crude Petroleum, Natural Gas and Natural Gasoline." These corporations account for about one-third of the total oil and gas produced at home and abroad by corporations filing United States income tax returns.[164] Net incomes reported for income tax purposes were adjusted for the approximate excess of depletion allowed over cost basis depletion and of intangible development expenses over book amortization of such expenses.[165] Rates of return for the oil and gas producing corporations were compared with those for all manufacturing corporations reporting net income and filing balance sheets with their income tax returns, except corporations engaged in producing petroleum and coal products. It was found that for the years covered the average rate of return on stockholders' equity was 24.2 per-

---

[162] *Oil and Gas Journal*, Annual Review and Outlook issues.

[163] McDonald, "Percentage Depletion and the Allocation of Resources" pp. 323–36, especially pp. 333–36.

[164] See note 56.

[165] See McDonald, "Percentage Depletion and the Allocation of Resources," pp. 328–29 and p. 334 for an explanation of the adjustment made.

cent for the oil and gas producing corporations and 12.0 percent for the manufacturing corporations. Corresponding rates of return on total capital, interest paid to creditors being treated as net income subject to the corporation tax, were 20.2 percent and 10.3 percent respectively.[166] Adjustment for debt in capital structures thus appears to make no difference in relative rates of return.

It will be noted that the computed average rate of return on stockholders' equity in manufacturing corporations is quite similar to the average in the same years for manufacturing corporations in the First National City Bank tabulation. But the rates of return for oil and gas producing corporations computed from income tax returns data are markedly higher than those indicated by the First National City Bank tabulation. Some part of this difference may arise from over-compensation of income tax data for the excess of tax charges over book charges. More important, undoubtedly, is the different composition of the two samples. Since publication of these data, the author has learned that the incomes represented in the Internal Revenue Service category of "Crude Petroleum, Natural Gas and Natural Gasoline" apparently are strongly influenced by earnings on foreign production. This category and another identified as "Oil and Gas Field Contract Services" make up a division in the IRS compilations designated "Crude Petroleum and Natural Gas Production." In the tax year 1956–57 there were 2,451 corporation income tax returns in this division, reporting a total net income of $630 million and an income tax liability of $294 million. Eighty-one of these returns were accompanied by claims for foreign tax credit. These 81 returns reported a total net income of $463 million, income tax liability of $234 million and foreign tax credit claimed in the amount of $194 million.[167] If for the years 1949–58 the corporation income tax returns of producers whose foreign tax credit was 90 percent or more of United States income tax liability are subtracted from total returns in the IRS category of "Crude Petroleum, Natural Gas and Natural Gasoline," the average rate of return on stockholders' equity drops from 19.5 percent to 12.3 percent. A similar adjustment for only those firms reporting net income results in a reduction of the average rate of return on stockholders' equity from 24.2

[166] *Ibid.*, pp. 334–35.

[167] U. S. Treasury Department, *Statistics of Income*, 1956–57, Part 2, pp. 84 and 106. It may be useful to add that in the same tax year foreign tax credits claimed by corporations in the "Petroleum and Coal Products" classification amounted to slightly more than one-third of income tax liability before credits. In the "Manufacturing" classification at large, the corresponding ratio was only about 5 percent. (*Ibid.*, pp. 84–85 and 106.)

percent to 16.2 percent.[168] These facts are consistent with the evidence from other sources that rates of return on foreign production tend to be higher than those on domestic production.[169] It may be, then, that for different reasons neither the estimates of the present writer nor those of the First National City Bank can be accepted without reservation as indicative of rates of return on domestic finding-developing-producing activities.[170] They both are consistent with the proposition that such rates of return tend to be higher than in manufacturing, other phases of the oil and gas industry, or all industry taken together, but they do not prove it. Further investigation is needed to put the proposition on a sufficiently firm basis.

Even if one is willing to agree that rates of return for the past twenty years have been relatively high in the finding-developing-producing phase of the domestic oil and gas industry, it may be argued that the persistent differential is due to relatively restricted competition in the industry. There appears to be no adequate basis for such an argument. Indeed, if anything, the contrary is more easily sustained. In perhaps the most thorough and authoritative study of the subject ever undertaken, McKie concludes that effective competition exists in the oil and gas industry, neither concentration nor barriers to entry offering "artificial impediments to the optimum adjustment of discovery to demand in the long run."[171] Scarcely anyone would argue that entry into the producing phase of the oil and gas industry is more difficult than entry into refining; and refining is one of the less concentrated of major manufacturing industries.[172] While, as in the case of risk, it is difficult to compare ease of

[168] Eldridge, *op. cit.*, p. 215. It has since been ascertained (from the Statistics Division, Internal Revenue Service) that eliminating from the category all returns with foreign tax credit claims makes no significant further difference in indicated rates of return.

[169] For instance, Wayne E. Leeman, *The Price of Middle East Oil* (Cornell University Press, 1962), pp. 69–78.

[170] Since percentage depletion applies to foreign as well as domestic production of oil and gas, the risks of foreign production are germane to the issue of percentage depletion. However, due to the physical, political, and market circumstances under which oil and gas are produced abroad by American companies, it would be extremely difficult to make a case for the proposition that the higher rates earned abroad simply reflect correspondingly higher risks abroad.

[171] McKie, *op. cit.*, pp. 570–71.

[172] As of 1954, petroleum refining ranked 209 in a total of 447 four-digit manufacturing industries arrayed in descending order of percent of total value of shipments accounted for by the four largest companies. In that year, the four largest companies in petroleum refining accounted for 32 percent of the industry's total value of shipments; the eight largest, 56 percent; and the twenty largest, 83 percent. (*Concentration in American Industry*, Report of the Subcommittee on Antitrust and Monopoly to the Com-

entry into different industries, the contrast in relevant circumstances between the refining and producing phases of the industry suggests that the producing phase is relatively easier to enter. Refining requires rather large aggregations of capital, a site with particular locational qualities, access to patentable processes, and highly skilled technicians and workers. In contrast, investments in the search for and production of oil and gas are highly divisible, and any needed skills, techniques, and devices can be had on a fee basis. Due to widespread deposits of oil and gas and the ease of transporting these raw minerals, there is no effective limit to the number of economical sites for an undertaking. A steady flow of entrepreneurs is provided by the "defection" of skilled and knowledgeable personnel from the major firms. Outside capital—from movie stars, physicians and others willing to risk some money that is subject to high marginal income tax rates—readily finds needy entrepreneurs through promoters specializing in such brokerage. State regulation offers no hindrance to exploration and development (quite the contrary!), but rather assures a share of the market to all who can establish production.[173] Yet the available data indicate that the rate of return in the finding-developing-producing phase of the industry has remained well above that in the refining phase for a

---

mittee on the Judiciary, U. S. Senate, 85 Cong. 1 sess., Committee Print [July 12, 1957], pp. 133–45. Underlying data from 1954 Census of Manufactures.) No strictly comparable data have been officially compiled for oil and gas production. However, Cookenboo reports that in 1952, the four largest producers accounted for 24 percent of gross domestic crude oil production; the eight largest, 41 percent; and the nineteen largest, 60 percent. (Leslie Cookenboo, Jr., *Crude Oil Pipelines and Competition in the Oil Industry* [Harvard University Press, 1955], p. 71.) Actually, the relevant concern here is freedom of entry into the industry; and concentration of production is not necessarily a good index of such freedom, particularly in the oil and gas industry, where it is an easy and widespread practice for major integrated companies to assure themselves of dependable and accessible refinery raw materials by purchasing producing properties discovered and developed by others.

[173] In Chapter V the market effects of state production regulation in the name of conservation are discussed in some detail. It is sometimes supposed that because such regulation tends to support prices, it also tends to protect rates of return in the industry. This supposition overlooks the well known principle that even a genuine cartel (which the system of state production regulation is not, despite certain resemblances) that cannot or does not restrict entry cannot protect members' rates of return. Particularly if its price support activity is geared to the needs of the weakest members, a cartel without restrictions on entry can only preside over the equalization of rates of return among members at a level (in equilibrium) that neither attracts capital from, nor repels it to, other pursuits. State conservation regulations offer no barriers to entry. By assuring entrants a share of the market and by creating a degree of price stability favorable to loan financing, such regulations probably tend to encourage entry.

period of time more than long enough to allow equilibrating reallocations of capital between the two phases.[174]

It should be emphasized that the foregoing discussion does not *prove* that the production of oil and gas is a relatively risky industry. It can be said, however, that available data on comparative rates of return, while far from satisfactory for the purposes at hand, are consistent with the proposition that typical investors regard the industry as relatively risky. The relative riskiness argument therefore cannot, in the author's opinion, be rejected without further investigation.

[174] The comparison in Table A-1 above probably understates the difference between rates of return in the finding-developing-producing phase and other phases of the oil and gas industry (principally refining). As explained in connection with presentation of the data in Table A-1, rates of return for corporations engaged in "integrated operations" reflect most of this country's oil and gas production and an even larger absolute quantity of foreign production.

Harberger's Model and the Allocative Effects of Differential Taxation

The effects on allocation of resources of differential taxation are demonstrated in an algebraic model developed by Arnold C. Harberger.[175] An adaptation of Harberger's model is presented here.

Without any income tax, the present worth of a machine (R_1) and the present worth of a mineral deposit (R_2) would both be equal to dY, where Y is the expected stream of income from each of them, net of all costs except depreciation and depletion, and d is a discount factor common to both of them taking the form of the ratio of present worth to absolute amount of income stream. (The higher is the rate of discount and the more delayed in time is the weighted average receipt, the lower is d.) With equal effective income tax rates, resulting from the same nominal tax rate (t) and both depreciation and depletion distributed in time in the same way as Y,

(1) $$R_1 = dY - td(Y - R_1), \quad \text{and}$$

(2) $$R_2 = dY - td(Y - R_2).$$

The expressions for R_1 and R_2 both reduce to $dY(1-t)/1-td$; consequently, R_1 remains equal to R_2. But suppose instead that the cost of the mineral deposit is tax-deductible as incurred and in addition the owner

[175] Harberger, *op. cit.* in note 58. See also pp. 49–52.

of the mineral deposit may make a special deduction equal to the fraction p of Y. The expression for R_2 now becomes:

(3)
$$R_2 = dY - t(dY - R_2 - pdY)$$
$$= \frac{dY(1 - t + tp)}{1 - t}.$$

It is readily apparent that R_2 is now larger than R_1. The numerator of the expression for R_2 is larger than that of the expression for R_1 on account of the special deduction (p); and the denominator is smaller on account of expensing, rather than amortizing, the cost of the mineral deposit.

In the above equations, the use of p as a percentage of cash flow rather than of gross income is a matter of algebraic convenience only. There is no misrepresentation of reality in this procedure, since some given absolute percentage depletion deduction is merely expressed as a fraction of cash flow rather than of gross income. (The cash flow fraction in reality is ordinarily larger than the effective rate of percentage depletion based on gross income, of course.) But there *is* misrepresentation of reality in treating the entire cost of a mineral property as subject to expensing at the time of the outlay. Some costs may be expensed as incurred, some may be charged off at various stages of an exploration program, some are recoverable through depreciation and some may not be separately deducted at all under the percentage depletion option. Following Steiner[176] let a_1, a_2, b and c represent the proportions of these four categories of costs, respectively ($a_1 + a_2 + b + c = 1$). The expression for the present worth of the mineral deposit (oil and gas) becomes:

(4)
$$R_2 = \frac{dY(1 - t + tp)}{1 - t(a_1 + d^*a_2 + db)},$$

where d^* is the discount factor pertinent to the peculiar time distribution of charge-offs represented in a_2. The category of costs represented by c has no place in the expression, since these costs are not separately deductible from gross income. Since a_1, a_2 and b add up to less than unity, and since d^* may be less than d, the denominator of the equation immediately above is not necessarily smaller than $1 - td$, although in reality it ordinarily is. The denominator *is* necessarily larger than $1 - t$; hence R_2 in (4) is smaller than R_2 in (3).

[176] Steiner, *op. cit.* p. 960.

Harberger's Model and the Price Effects of Differential Risk and Capital Turnover

With the addition of a term to indicate capital turnover, the basic Harberger model[177] may be used to illustrate the relative price effects of differential risk and differential capital turnover under the assumptions used in the author's model. Assume that before an income tax is imposed the present worths of two assets corresponding to the two industries being compared are equal. Thus:

$$R_1 = R_2 = d_1 Y_1 = d_2 Y_2$$

where

R = present worth (and cost) of income stream,
d = discount factor reflecting rate of return, period and time-shape of income stream,
Y = undiscounted income stream net of all costs except capital consumption and income taxes.

In the absence of tax, then, the two assets would be equally attractive to prospective investors. Let Industry (2) be the riskier industry, so that d_2 is smaller than d_1. The cash flow of Industry (2) is correspondingly larger than that of Industry (1), reflecting the larger proportion of net income to capital consumption. Now let an income tax be equally imposed, each industry depreciating its asset according to a time schedule identical with

---

[177] Harberger *op. cit.* See also pp. 49–52.

that of the receipt of Y. The present worths now become:

$$R_1' = \frac{d_1 Y_1 (1 - t)}{1 - td_1} \quad \text{and} \quad R_2' = \frac{d_2 Y_2 (1 - t)}{1 - td_2} .$$

The numerators of these fractions are equal, but the denominator in the second case is larger, since d_2 is smaller than d_1. Hence $R_2' < R_1'$.

For a new equilibrium to be achieved, under the assumptions of the present writer's model, the initial values of R_1 and R_2 must be restored through upward adjustments of Y_1 and Y_2, hence of product prices in the two industries. Specifically,

Y_1 must be increased by the factor,

$$\frac{1 - td_1}{1 - t} ,$$

and

Y_2 must be increased by the factor,

$$\frac{1 - td_2}{1 - t} .$$

The latter factor is larger than the former factor, since d_2 is smaller than d_1. Moreover, the proportionate increase in the *product prices* of Industry (2) will be larger still if capital turnover in that industry is less than that in Industry (1). Thus,

let

$$\frac{G_1}{Y_1} = a \cdot \frac{G_2}{Y_2}$$

where

G = gross receipts from sales and
a = a multiplier greater than 1.

So long as Y_2 is less than aY_1 this condition implies that capital turnover is greater in Industry (1) than in Industry (2), since R_1 equals R_2 in equilibrium and the schedule of capital consumption is the same for the two industries. [The average amount of capital employed per dollar of sales is less in Industry (1) than in Industry (2).] Accordingly,

product prices in Industry (1) must be increased by the factor,

$$\frac{1 - td_1}{a(1 - t)} \cdot \frac{Y_2}{G_2}$$

and

product prices in Industry (2) must be increased by the factor,

$$\frac{1 - td_2}{1 - t} \cdot \frac{Y_2}{G_2} \ .$$

It is obvious that the latter factor is larger than the former factor because d_2 is smaller than d_1 and $(1 - t)$ is smaller than $a(1 - t)$.

APPENDIX D

Increasing Costs of Replacement

Although it is reasonable to expect that at some stage in its development the United States oil and gas industry might become subject to increasing real costs of replacement, it is uncertain whether the stage has
already been reached. The author is unaware of any truly satisfactory
demonstration of a tendency toward increasing costs in this country, even
in recent years. It can be shown that physical discoveries, particularly of
crude oil, per well or per foot drilled have been declining over the past
decade or so,[178] but this is not necessarily an indication of increasing real
costs. Technological improvements in drilling may have offset the cost
effects of greater footage per physical unit discovered. Overdrilling induced by patterns of state conservation regulation and the distinctive tax
provisions (see Chapter V) may account for the growth of drilling footage
relative to discoveries. Natural gas discoveries, which are growing in relative importance, must be meaningfully combined with crude oil discoveries
before costs are weighed against results. The overdrilling problem aside,
to make an adequate comparison of real costs and results one needs on
the cost side a measure of real capital outlays for proving the existence
and quantity of reserves of all kinds—crude oil, natural gas and natural
gas liquids.

The Chase-Manhattan Bank annually makes an authoritative estimate
of total capital outlays by the industry, but the published data unfortunately lump natural gas transmission and distribution outlays with outlays

[178] Mid-Continent Oil and Gas Association, *op. cit.*, p. 16.

153

for exploration and development proper.[179] Even if such extraneous outlays were removed, there would remain the question of development outlays on such items as pumps, tanks and service wells that may or may not be pertinent in proving the existence and quantity of reserves. Finally, a suitable price index is required to deflate the outlay series.

On the results side of the comparison, one needs a measure of discovered reserves that properly credits extensions and revisions to the years in which pertinent outlays were made. The author is unaware of the existence of any such measure. Published data[180] combine revisions of previous estimates with current-year discoveries, a procedure which makes it difficult to interpret the results of current year outlays. Since exploration is indivisible as between oil and gas results, discoveries of oil and gas need to be combined in some economically meaningful way to enable a significant comparison of costs and results. Use of relative B.T.U. content as the common denominator for such a combination is less than satisfactory, for a B.T.U. has a different economic significance in the form of gas than in the form of crude oil. A better common denominator would be relative discovery value, but data for such a measure would be virtually impossible to secure on a systematic, reliable basis, partly because discovery value per unit depends in part on the number of units believed to have been discovered. It thus appears that the question of increasing real costs of finding oil and gas is a difficult one, on which no definite conclusion seems possible at this time.[181]

---

[179] For annual data running back to 1946, see American Petroleum Institute. *Petroleum Facts and Figures* (1959), p. 412, citing Petroleum Department, The Chase-Manhattan Bank.

[180] American Petroleum Institute, *op. cit.*, p. 62.

[181] For a thorough analysis of the problem of measuring and interpreting oil finding costs see Wallace F. Lovejoy and Paul T. Homan (with Charles O. Galvin), "Cost Analysis in the Petroleum Industry," *Journal of the Graduate Research Center*, Southern Methodist University (February 1963).

A Selected Bibliography

American Petroleum Institute, *Petroleum Facts and Figures*. New York, 1959.

American Petroleum Institute, Independent Petroleum Association of America, and Mid-Continent Oil and Gas Association, *Joint Association Survey: Estimated Expenditures and Receipts of U. S. Oil and Gas Producing Industry, 1959*. New York, 1960.

———, *Joint Association Survey of Industry Drilling Costs, 1959*. New York, 1960.

Baker, Rex G., and Erwin N. Griswold, "Percentage Depletion—A Correspondence," *Harvard Law Review*, Vol. 64, January 1951.

Blaise, F. J., "What Every Tax Man Should Know About Percentage Depletion," *Taxes: The Tax Magazine*, Vol. 36, June 1958.

Brock, Horace R., *Accounting for Leasehold, Exploration and Development Costs in the American Petroleum Industry*, unpublished doctoral thesis, Austin: The University of Texas, 1954.

Buckley, S. E., ed., *Petroleum Conservation*. Dallas: American Institute of Mining and Metallurgical Engineers, 1951.

Ciriacy-Wantrup, S. V., *Resource Conservation: Economics and Policies*. Berkeley: University of California Press, 1952.

Cookenboo, Leslie, Jr., *Crude Oil Pipelines and Competition in the Oil Industry*. Cambridge: Harvard University Press, 1955.

Creamer, Daniel, and others, *Capital in Manufacturing and Mining*. National Bureau of Economic Research. Princeton: Princeton University Press, 1960.

Davidson, Paul, "Policy Problems of the Crude Oil Industry," *American Economic Review*, Vol. 53, March 1963.

Dean, Joel, *Managerial Economics*. New York: Prentice-Hall, 1956.

de Chazeau, M. G. and A. E. Kahn, *Integration and Competition in the Petroleum Industry*. New Haven: Yale University Press, 1959.

Eldridge, Douglas H., "Rate of Return, Resource Allocation and Percentage Depletion," *National Tax Journal*, Vol. 15, June 1962.

Galvin, Charles O., "The 'Ought' and 'Is' of Oil-and-Gas Taxation," *Harvard Law Review*, Vol. 73, June 1960.

Goode, Richard, *The Corporation Income Tax*. New York: John Wiley and Sons, 1951.

Grayson, C. Jackson, *Decisions Under Uncertainty: Drilling Decisions by Oil and Gas Operators*. Boston: Harvard Graduate School of Business Administration, 1960.

Harberger, Arnold C., "The Corporation Income Tax: An Empirical Appraisal," *Tax Revision Compendium*, Vol. 1, U. S. Congress, House Committee on Ways and Means, Committee Print. Washington, 1959.

————, "The Incidence of the Corporation Income Tax," *Journal of Political Economy*, Vol. 70, June 1962.

————, "The Taxation of Mineral Industries," in *Federal Tax Policy for Economic Growth and Stability*, U. S. Congress, Joint Committee on the Economic Report, Committee Print. Washington, 1955.

Hardwicke, R. E., "Oil-Well Spacing Regulations and Protection of Property Rights in Texas, "*Texas Law Review*, Vol. 31, December 1952.

Hart, Albert G., *Anticipations, Uncertainty and Dynamic Planning*. New York: Augustus M. Kelley, 1951.

Knight, Frank H., *Risk, Uncertainty and Profit*. Boston: Houghton-Mifflin, 1921.

Lentz, Oscar H., "Mineral Economics and the Problem of Equitable Taxation," *Quarterly of the Colorado School of Mines*, Vol. 55, April 1960.

Lichtblau, John H., and Dillard P. Spriggs, *The Oil Depletion Issue*. New York: Petroleum Industry Research Foundation, 1959.

Lovejoy, Wallace F. and Paul T. Homan (with Charles O. Galvin), "Cost Analysis in the Petroleum Industry," *Journal of the Graduate Research Center*, Southern Methodist University, February 1963.

Lovejoy, Wallace F. and James I. Pikl (eds.), *Essays on Petroleum Conservation Regulation*, Dallas: Southern Methodist University, 1960.

Manning, Raymond E., *Depletion Allowances Under Federal Income Tax and Allowances for Exploration and Development Costs (Pro and Con Discussion)*. Washington: Library of Congress, Legislative Reference Service, 1959.

McDonald, Stephen L., "Percentage Depletion and the Allocation of Resources: The Case of Oil and Gas," *National Tax Journal*, Vol. 14, December 1961.

————, "Percentage Depletion and Tax Neutrality: A Reply to Messrs. Musgrave and Eldridge," *National Tax Journal*, Vol. 15, September 1962.

McKie, James W., "Market Structure and Uncertainty in Oil and Gas Exploration," *Quarterly Journal of Economics*, Vol. 74, November 1960.

McKie, James W. and Stephen L. McDonald, "Petroleum Conservation in Theory and Practice," *Quarterly Journal of Economics*, Vol. 76, February 1962.

Mid-Continent Oil and Gas Association, *Percentage Depletion and Its Appropriate Rate*. Tulsa, 1957.

————, *Percentage Depletion, Economic Progress, and National Security*. Tulsa, 1961.

Musgrave, Richard A., "Another Look at Depletion," *National Tax Journal*, Vol. 15, June 1962.

————, *The Theory of Public Finance*. New York: McGraw-Hill, 1959.

Oil and Gas Journal, Annual Review Issues, various years.

Rostow, E. V., *A National Policy for the Oil Industry*. New Haven: Yale University Press, 1948.

Scott, Anthony, *Natural Resources: The Economics of Conservation*. Toronto: University of Toronto Press, 1955.

Seltzer, Lawrence H., *The Nature and Treatment of Capital Gains and Losses*. National Bureau of Economic Research. Princeton: Princeton University Press, 1951.

Standard Oil Company of New Jersey, *An Analysis of the Depletion Provision as it Applies to the Petroleum Industry*. New York, 1958.

Steiner, Peter O., "Percentage Depletion and Resource Allocation," *Tax Revision Compendium*, Vol. 2, U. S. Congress, House Committee on Ways and Means, Committee Print. Washington, 1959.

U. S. Congress. House of Representatives. Committee on Ways and Means. Hearings, 81 Cong. 2 sess. Feb. 3, 1950. Washington, 1950.

————. ————. ————. "Percentage Depletion and Exploration and Development Costs," *Tax Revision Compendium*, Vol. 2, Section G-2, Committee Print. Washington, 1959. Papers reproduced:

Charles O. Galvin, "The Deduction for Percentage Depletion and Exploration and Development Costs."

Peter O. Steiner, "Percentage Depletion and Resource Allocation."

John Menge, "The Role of Taxation in Providing for Depletion of Mineral Reserves."

Horace M. Gray, "Tax Reform and the Depletion Allowance."

Harry J. Rudick, "Depletion and Exploration and Development Costs."

Richard J. Gonzalez, "Percentage Depletion for Petroleum Production."

Scott C. Lambert, "Percentage Depletion and Exploration and Development Costs."

Herbert C. Jackson, "Depletion and Exploration Expenses."

L. J. Randall, "Depletion and Exploration and Development Costs of the Mining Industry."

Rolla D. Campbell, "Percentage Depletion and Exploration and Development Costs."

————. Joint Committee on the Economic Report. "Impact of Federal Taxation on Natural Resources Development," *Federal Tax Policy for Economic Growth and Stability*, Section 9, Committee Print. Washington, 1955. Papers reproduced:

Henry B. Fernald, "Distinctive Tax Treatment of Income from Mineral Extraction."

Horace M. Gray, "Percentage Depletion, Conservation, and Economic Structure."

Arnold C. Harberger, "Taxation of Mineral Industries."

Scott C. Lambert, "Percentage Depletion and National Interest."

James R. Nelson, "Percentage Depletion and National Security."

Arthur A. Smith, "Tax Policy as Reflected in Statutory Percentage Depletion for Oil and Gas."

Lowell Stanley, "The Independent Producer's Position."

————. Joint Committee on Internal Revenue Taxation. *Legislative History of Depletion Allowances.* Staff Report for Use of the House Committee on Ways and Means. Washington: Government Printing Office, 1950.

————. Joint Economic Committee, *The Federal Revenue System: Facts and Problems. 1961.* Washington: Government Printing Office, 1961.

————. Senate. Subcommittee on Antitrust and Monopoly of the Committee on the Judiciary. *Concentration in American Industry.* 85 Cong. 1 sess. Committee Print. Washington, 1957.

U. S. Department of Commerce. Bureau of the Census. *1958 Census of Mineral*

Industries, Industry and Product Reports: Crude Petroleum and Natural Gas. Washington, 1960.

U. S. Department of the Interior, Bureau of Mines. *Minerals Yearbook.* Washington, various years.

U. S. Treasury Department. Internal Revenue Service, *Statistics of Income, Part 2, Corporation Income Tax Returns,* for years 1949–56. Washington: 1951–58.

Watkins, M. W., *Oil: Stabilization or Conservation?* New York: Harper, 1937.

Wilkinson, J. Henry, Jr., "ABC—From A to Z," *Texas Law Review,* Vol. 38, June 1960.

———, "ABC Transactions and Related Income Tax Plans," *Texas Law Review,* Vol. 40, November 1961.

Zimmermann, Erich W., *Conservation in the Production of Petroleum.* New Haven: Yale University Press, 1957.

Index

"ABC deal," 98–99

Accounting practices, internal: and measures of capital consumption, 68; and rates of return, 123; and risk comparisons, 46, 47, 55; vs. tax return practices, 22

Aggregation of properties (*see also* Productive property): effect on allowable depletion, 21n

Allocation of resources. *See* Resource allocation.

Amerada Petroleum Corporation, 36, 37

American Petroleum Institute, 35n, 103n

Amortization of costs: "double-declining-balance" formula, 25–26; vs. expensing, 23–26

Anderson, C. C., 18n, 32n

Austin, W. Leo, 15n

Blaise, F. J., 11n

Brock, Horace R., 22n

Buckley, S. E., 73n, 77n

Business fluctuations and the demand for oil and gas. *See under* Elasticity of demand for oil and gas

Byrd, Harry F., 111, 112n

California, lack of oil conservation law, 77n, 78, 80

Capital: differences in intensity of, 2, 3, 60, 64, 81, 120, 121; elasticity of supply of, 58–59; and net income, 65–68; substitution of labor for, 53, 59; theory of, and conservation, 53, 59; turnover, rate of, 54–58, 61n, 63, 64, 104, 150–52

Capital consumption (*see also* Cost depletion; Distinctive tax provision; Percentage depletion; Wasting assets), 17, 24, 94; measures of, 67–70, 72

Capital gains tax: and the distinctive tax provisions, 2, 5, 6, 13, 115; and the sale of oil and gas properties, 92–100, 115–16, 119, 134, 136, 137; value of, in oil and gas industry, 93–98

Capital outlays: as costs of production, 122; expensing of, 2, 23n, 61n, 72, 100, 129, 134–36; related to value of assets, 11, 15, 66–69, 70n, 71, 72; and risk, 27–28, 61

Capital-output ratio, effect of tax on, 59, 61n

Carsey, J. Ben, 41

Ciriacy-Wantrup, S. V., 73, 73n, 74, 74n

Conservation of oil and gas, 2, 4; definition of, 73–74, 128–29; and the distinctive tax provisions, 4, 77, 79, 81–83, 119, 128–29; "market demand" regulation, 43, 74n, 78–81, 89, 90n, 102, 132; state regulation of, 4, 44, 74, 77–81, 82, 82n, 83, 88–89, 91, 126, 129–31; stock and flow resources, 74–75; well density, 77–80, 82n, 83, 89, 109, 110, 129; and the theory of capital, 74, 75

Cookenboo, Leslie, Jr., 146n

Corporation income tax. *See* Income tax.

Cost of asset: as basis for capital consumption allowances, 70–72; related to value, 11, 15, 66–69, 70n, 71, 72

Cost depletion (*see also* Distinctive tax provisions; Percentage depletion), 1, 9–11, 13–15, 17, 34n, 70–72, 94, 96; and disaggregation of properties, 21n; and percentage depletion, relative advantages of, 16–19, 21–22, 94, 96, 98–100, 137; proposed limit on, 134, 136–37

159